I0519205

Septuagint:

Judges and Ruth

Septuagint, Volume 7

SCRIPTURAL RESEARCH INSTITUTE
Published by Digital Ink Productions, 2024

Copyright

While every precaution has been taken in the preparation of this book, the publisher assumes no responsibility for errors or omissions, or for damages resulting from the use of the information contained herein.

Septuagint: Judges and Ruth

Second edition. February 21, 2024

Copyright © 2024 Scriptural Research Institute.

ISBN: 978-1-998288-48-9

The Septuagint was translated into Greek at the Library of Alexandria between 250 and 132 BC.

This English translation was created by the Scriptural Research Institute in 2019 through 2024, through the comparison of most published copies of Septuagint manuscripts. Additionally, the Leningrad Codex of the Masoretic text, Peshitta, Coptic, Ge'ez, and Armenian Bibles, Targums, and Dead Sea Scrolls were used for comparative analysis.

The image used for the cover is an artistic reinterpretation of 'Samson and Delilah' by José Echenagusía Errazkin, painted in 1887. The original painting is currently located at the Bilbao Fine Arts Museum, in Bilbao.

Table of Contents

TABLE OF CONTENTS

TABLE OF CONTENTS

Forward

In the mid 3rd century BC, King Ptolemy II Philadelphus of Egypt ordered a translation of the ancient Israelite scriptures for the Library of Alexandria. This translation later became known as the Septuagint, based on the description of the translation by seventy translators in the Letter of Aristeas. The original version, published circa 250 BC, only included the Torah, or in Greek terms, the Pentateuch. The Torah is the five books traditionally credited to Moses, circa 1500 BC: Cosmic Genesis, Exodus, Leviticus, Numbers, and Deuteronomy. According to Jewish tradition, the original Torah was lost when the Babylonians destroyed the Temple of Solomon, and it was then rewritten by Ezra the Scribe from memory during the Second Temple period.

The first edition was followed by the second, around 225 BC which added the books of Joshua, Judges, and Ruth, which was later known as the Octateuch. This version of the Septuagint was later carried south into the Kingdom of Kush by the Israelites fleeing Egypt in 200 BC when Judea was in revolt and the Ptolemys attempted to exterminate the Israelites in Egypt. The Octateuch later became the Torah of the Beta Israel community in Sudan and Ethiopia known as the Orit.

It is generally accepted that there were several versions written in Phoenician (Samaritan or Judahite) or Aramaic before the translation of the Septuagint. Fragments of the book of Judges have been found among the dead sea scrolls, however, only in the Assyrian (Aramaic) script of the Hasmonean Dynasty, and dated to between 140 and 37 BC. By this time, the land of Judea passed from the rule of the Ptolemys in Egypt to the rule of the Seleucids in Syria in 200 BC. The Seleucids attempted to Hellenize the Judeans, and effectively banned traditional Judaism. This Hellenizing activity was partially successful, creating the Sadducee faction of Judaism, however also led to the Maccabean Revolt in 165 BC, which itself created the independent Hasmonean Kingdom of Judea. This kingdom was violently xenophobic and led by a priestly monarchy that combined both the powers of the state and the church.

The Hasmonean dynasty attempted to conquer all of the territory that had previously been part of the Persian Province of Judea, and either evicted or exterminated the people that were living there, depending on their ethnicity. When the Edomites were conquered they were allowed to mass-convert to Judaism as they were considered the descendants of Esau, however, most other ethnic groups were not welcome. When the army of Hasmonean King John Hyrcanus annexed Samaria in 113

BC, he slaughtered the Samaritan priests and more than half the Samaritan population and enslaved the rest. His army also destroyed the Samaritan Temple on Mount Gerizim and burned all copies of their holy books. The Samaritans continued to be slaves under the Hasmoneans until the Roman General Pompey's armies freed them in 69 BC, and restored the independent state of Samaria, along with several other states that fell under Rome's protection from that time forward.

While the Hasmoneans ruled Judea, they converted the national script from the old Canaanite script, today called Paleo-Hebrew, to the Assyrian 'block script,' today called Hebrew. As a result, almost all surviving texts found from the Hasmonean era and later are written in the Assyrian script, and it is unclear how much the Hasmoneans redacted the scriptures when they transcribed them. The scriptures the Hasmoneans left the world were later used as the basis of the Masoretic Text, which is used today by Rabbinical Jews, as well as by Catholic and Protestant Christians.

The Samaritan Torah is believed to have been restored after General Pompey freed the Samaritans, by redacting a copy of the Hasmonean Torah, which is why there are fewer differences between the Samaritan and Jewish (Masoretic) Torahs than either of them and the Septuagint. A copy of the original Samaritan Torah was translated at the Library of Alexandria as well, referred to as the Samareitikon (Σαμαρειτικον), however, it has not survived to the present. Based on the writings of Origen of Alexandria in the early 3rd century, and other early Christians, the Samareitikon was more similar to the Septuagint's Pentateuch than it was to either the Samaritan or Jewish Torahs in use at the time.

The differences between the Masoretic and the Septuagint's version of Joshua, and several other books in the two collections of scriptures are both minor and startling, as the two sets of scriptures contain the same stories, but different Gods. The God of the book of Judges in the Septuagint is called 'the Lord the god' (τον Κύριον τὸν θεὸν), or simplified to 'the lord' (τοῦ κυρίου). These terms are mirrored in the Masoretic version of Judges with 'the Yehwah god' (אֶת־יְהוָה אֱלֹהֵי), and the name Yhvah (יְהוָה). One explanation for the difference between the texts is the Christian redaction of the 3rd century AD, when the name Iaô (Ιαω) was removed from the Septuagint, replaced by Lord (Κύριοσ).

Fragments of older Septuagint manuscripts still exist that contain the name Iaô (Ιαω), transliterated from the Aramaic Yhw (𐤉𐤄𐤅), however, none of the fragments of the Book of Judges include the name. The name Yhwh (יהוה) is found in a couple of fragments of Judges found among the Dead Sea Scrolls, however, they date to the

Hasmonean dynasty, and therefore date to over 85 years after the Septuagint's version of Judges was translated.

The Aramaic sections of Masoretic Daniel that were not translated into Hebrew maintain the term adonai ha'elohim (אֲדֹנָי הָאֱלֹהִים), meaning the 'Lord the gods' where the Septuagint has 'Lord the god' (Κύριον τὸν θεὸν), however, the Hebrew sections have Yehvah elohim (יְהוָה אֱלֹהִים) where the Septuagint has 'Lord the god,' suggesting the Greek more accurately reflects the Aramaic source texts than the Hebrew translation. According to the Talmud, this was to repair the damage King Manasseh had done 600 years earlier when he removed the name Yhwh from the Israelite Texts, however, no evidence has survived from the era of Manasseh or earlier that proves the name was originally in the text, suggesting it was an attempt by the first Hasmonean High-Priest/King Simon the Zealot to create a national Judean religion with a god having a name similar to the Roman god Jove.

The Greek terms in the Septuagint's Judges are translations of well-known terms related to Canaanite god El, the Canaanite creator-god. El translates in Canaanite, Aramaic, and Hebrew as 'God,' and was the primary god worshiped in ancient Canaan in the era Abraham, Isaac, and Jacob were reported to have passed through the area. El was also the patron god of the Temple of El, built by

Jacob near the modern city of Nablus in the Palestinian West Bank, which featured in many of the early Hebrew scriptures before Samaria was conquered by the Assyrian Empire.

In the Book of Micah, the Temple of El was referred to as Jacob's Temple of El, which confirms that the Israelites in the 8th century BC considered the Temple of El at Shiloh to be the Temple of El that Jacob built in Genesis chapter 35. In Judges, the Temple of El in Shechem is called the fortified Temple of the God of the Covenant, and the Temple of the Lord of the Covenant in both the Septuagint and the Masoretic Text, which supports the identification of El with the covenant in the early Israelite religion.

The Septuagint's book of Joshua, the book directly preceding Judges in the Octateuch, has the first reference to Sabaoth (Σαβαωθ) in chapter 6, as Lord Sabaoth (Κυρίω Σαβαωθ). Sabaoth would later become the god of the Hasmonean dynasty as part of the name Yehvah tzeva'ovt (יְהוָה צְבָאֹות). The Hebrew word transliterated as Sabaoth, which the Greeks and Romans treated as the proper name of the Hasmonean god, is a military term, roughly meaning 'army' or 'forces.' As such, the fusion of the Jewish god Iaw (Yhwh) with Sabaoth created a militaristic version of Iaw, a war-god, for a warrior-dynasty.

The Hasmoneans may have promoted Iaw Sabaoth, however, in Joshua, Saboath is not called Iaw Sabaoth, but Lord Sabaoth. This cannot be as a result of the Christian redaction of the name Iaw (Ιαω) in the 3rd century, as the Masoretic Text only have Yehvah, not Yehvah tzeva'ovt. This implies strongly that the Hasmoneans redacted Lord Sabaoth from Joshua when they transcribed it into the Assyrian 'Hebrew' script. If so, then they believed it was the name of one of the ancient Canaanite gods that they were removing from the sacred texts.

The Book of Judges also includes many other gods, which the ancient Israelites are repeatedly accused of worshiping, including Ba'al, Asherah, and the Lords (Baalim) and Ashteroths of the Canaanites. Several of the Canaanite gods are mentioned incidentally, such as the fertility god Lord Lahem, the god of dusk Lord Shalim, the solar-god Lord Shemesh, and the grain-god Dagon. All these gods are part of the old Canaanite religion, in which El (God) and his wife Asherah (commonly called Qetesh) were the parents of the Canaanite gods. The term ba'al translates as lord, however, when used as a name, it generally represented Lord Hadad, the storm god of the Ba'al Cycle literature of the ancient Ugaritic texts in ancient Canaan. The Ugaritic Texts continued to be used well into the era of the ancient kingdoms of

Samaria and Judah, as the prophet Jeremiah quoted them circa 630 BC. Additionally, the name of the Egyptian god Aten appears to have been in the Book of Judges before Aten was forgotten as a god. The name appears twice, once in the Song of Deborah, in chapter 5, and later as part of the name of a town in chapter 12:

> "You who move as Aten the sun god at midday, sitting in judgment, and following the path, and riding the pathway, declare from the noise of disturbers among the drawers of water, and retell the righteous acts of the Lord. Increase righteous acts in Israel, then the people of the Lord will go down to the cities."

> "After him, Abdon the son of Hillel, a Per-Atenite, judged Israel. He had forty sons, and thirty grandsons, that rode on seventy colts, and he judged Israel eight years. Abdon the son of Hillel, the Per-Atenite, died and was buried in Per-Aten in the land of Ephraim in the mountains of Amalek."

In both cases, a word that appears to be a transliteration of Aten survives in the Masoretic Text, although is considered an unknown term, and has been viewed that way for thousands of years. The Book of Judges contains more unknown terms than any other book in the Masoretic Text and the most archaic form of Canaanite other than in the Book of Job. Judges is considered by most biblical scholars to be the oldest book in the

Masoretic Text, composed earlier than the surviving versions of the Torah, or Joshua.

Nevertheless, the version in the Masoretic Text still suffers from the damage done by the Hasmonean dynasty and therefore does not align with the recorded history of the Egyptians, Assyrians, or Babylonians, causing many historians to consider it to be a collection of very ancient fictional stories. On the other hand, the Septuagint's version of Exodus, Joshua, and Judges, contain a different chronology from the Masoretic text, covering 460 years from the time of the Exodus, circa 1550 BC, to the era of chaos that started in 1090 BC, and would later end in 1037 BC when Saul became the first king of the independent Kingdom of Israel.

Saul was not the first king of the Israelites, as Abimelech had previously been recognized as King of Israel a couple of centuries earlier. Abimelech's reign had only been for three years and seems to have only controlled the region around Shechem, the city that would later become the capital of Saul's Israel. This earlier attempt at an independent kingdom took place between 1267 and 1264 BC, according to the Septuagint, at the same time that the Egyptian records report that King Ramesses II had lost control over Canaan. The fact that the Egyptians dominated Canaan throughout the era of the Judges is not in doubt; Egyptian, Babylonian, Assyrian, and Nesite records all confirm this, as do the archaeological ruins of Egyptian cities spread through the region. The curious thing is that they are not mentioned in the book of Judges.

There is a reference to what appears to be a transliteration of 'Egypt' found in the Masoretic Text, however, it is for some reason assumed to be a village called 'Egypt' somewhere in Canaan. Like one of the earlier references to Aten, this reference to 'Egypt' is found in the Song of Deborah, in chapter 5:

"My mighty mind will trample him down. When the hoofs of the horse were entangled, his mighty ones earnestly rushed to curse Southern Egypt. Curse it," said the messenger of the lord.

The place that was cursed in this verse is generally transliterated as Meroz from the Masoretic Text, which is not new, as the Greeks transliterated it as Mêrôz (Μηρωζ) circa 225 BC, and Lucian of Antioch transliterated it as Marôz (Μαρωζ) circa 300 AD.

The question of what Meroz was, has resulted in a great deal of speculation. The commentary in the Talmud (Moed Katan 16a) claims that Meroz is a planet that refused to help the Israelites in their time of trouble, however, the name Meroz does not correlate with the Semitic name of any planet in this star system, and was likely an error based on the misidentification of the Latin name of the planet Mars during the Roman era. In the later school of Merkabah mysticism, Meroz became a class of angels that lived on the planet Meroz who refused to help the Israelites, instead of the planet itself, meaning in modern terms, Yehvah was cursing a group of extraterrestrials.

Modern scholarship has focused on the idea that there was a village in Israel called Misr, which is the Arabic name for Egypt. This village of Egyptians would then have been the focus of the curse, however, there is no known village called Misr dating to that time period, nor an explanation for the Arabic name. There is a village called Misr in northern modern Israel, however, it appears to have been founded much later.

The connection between Meroz and Misr is generally based on the assumption that Mrvz (מרוז) was a scribal error, a transcription error of Mtzr (מצר), however, it is difficult to see how that could have happened. Egypt was known as ᵐᵃᵗMuṣru (𒆳𒈨𒈬𒊒) in Akkadian, Miṣriåi (𒈫𒊑𒀀𒀀) in Babylonian, Mṣrm (𐎎𐎕𐎗𐎎) in Ugaritic, Mṣryn (𐡌𐡑𐡓𐡉𐡍) in Aramaic, Mitzrayim (מִצְרַיִם) in Hebrew, and Mitzr (مصر) in Arabic. The Mycenaean Greeks also used the adopted Semitic name as Misarajo (𐀖𐀭𐀬) . None of the known variants of the Semitic name of Egypt are a close match to Meroz/Maroz, however, the Egyptian name Marēs, is almost phonetically identical.

Måôresi (𓂋𓂝𓏤𓈖𓏏𓈉) was an ancient Egyptian name for Southern Egypt, which translates as approximately 'Southern Place.' It continued to be used until the Classical era, when it was spelled as Marēs (Μαρнϲ) in Coptic, the Classical form of Egyptian. The exact pronunciation of ancient Egyptian names is debated before the development of the Demotic script in the early Iron Age, and therefore it cannot be known how the Egyptians pronounced Mares during the era of Deborah, however, it is documented in Demotic as being Måôrs (ϥ/ⲟⲣⲥ), supporting the New Kingdom era pronunciation as being very similar to the term used by Deborah.

Nevertheless, the Song of Deborah does not curse a 'village of Meroz,' but 'Meroz' itself, meaning Southern Egypt. Meroz is cursed for not sending troops to help the Israelites during the era when King Jabin of Hazor was dominating the land, which according to the timeline of the Septuagint was a 20 year period between 1334 and 1314 BC. This was the era between the collapse of Egyptian power at the end of the Amarna Period, and the resurgence of Egyptian power under Pharaoh Horemheb. At the time, the capital of the Egyptian Empire was in Thebes, the capital of southern Egypt.

The Amarna Period, as Egyptologists call it, is the era when Pharaoh Amenhotep IV changed his name to Akhenaten, moved the capital of Egypt to a new city he built called Amarna, and instituted a national religion in Egypt today called Atenism. Under his rule, the various temples of the old gods of Egypt were systematically shut down, and a new national priesthood was created focused on the one god that all Egyptians could see every day, the sun, then known as Aten. His reign left the Empire in chaos, and when he died in 1336 BC, the empire rapidly shifted between the Pharaohs Smenkhkare (1335-1334 BC), Nefer-neferuaten (1334-1332 BC), and Tutankhamen (1334-1325 BC).

Pharaoh Tutankhamen was a boy when he assumed the throne, and the real power at the time appears to have been Ay, who would later become Pharaoh himself after Tutankhamen's young death left no heirs. Tutankhamen and Ay restored the priesthoods of the old gods, and abandoned Amarna, returning the imperial capital to Thebes. The priesthood of Aten quickly faded away, and Aten disappeared from the list of Egyptian gods, forgotten entirely until Egyptologists rediscovered him in the late 1800s. Ay ruled for just over a decade (1332-1319 BC), and managed to restore some semblance of normality to Upper and Lower Egypt, however, Kush and Canaan remained in chaos until Horemheb (1319-

1292 BC) reestablished Egyptian control early in his reign.

The Amarna Letters from the era describe the region being overrun, and the Canaanites repeatedly requesting aid from the government in Amarna, which never came. Most it the letters numbered between 200 and 300 are requests from local governors in Jerusalem and other Canaanite cities describing the situation as the Habirus switched sides, and various governors revolted from Egypt's rule.

This matches what is recorded in the book of Judges, where 80 years of peace under the Judges Ehud and Shamgar ended in 1334 BC when King Jabin of Hazor seized control of Canaan, supported by the Chief-of-the-army Siazara, who lived in the Forge-of-the-Foreigners, and commanded a force of 900 iron chariots. Based on both the Canaanite texts and Egyptian records Jabin was a common Canaanite name, however, Siazara appears to be the Egyptian name Siazårô (⟨𓄿𓃀𓇓𓏏𓇳⟩), meaning 'recognized son of Ra.' This specific name would have denoted a king from either southern Egypt or Nubia, however, Siazara is otherwise unknown from regal records, suggesting he attempted to seize control of the empire after Akhenaten died, however, ultimately failed, and was left out of the regal history of Egypt.

The 900 iron chariots are generally assumed to be an exaggeration, or a flat lie by scholars studying the book of Judges, as no petty Canaanite chieftain could have raised a force of 900 chariots at that time, and iron was generally not in use by armies until much later, after 1200 BC. This is, however, not exactly true. Tutankhamen was buried with an iron dagger in 1325 BC, and that dagger was of very high quality. Modern analysis indicates it may have been meteoric iron, however, it may have simply been made of the iron-nickel residue produced from the gold smelting in southeast Egypt.

Iron smelting was in use across the ancient world by the era of the Amarna Period, including in Anatolia, where the Hattic civilization had been smelting iron since at least 2500 BC, and in Uttar Pradesh, in India, where iron had been smelted since at least 1800 BC, however, in Egypt the high-quality iron-nickel weapons and jewelry found by Egyptologists are believed to have been made from the residue of gold smelting and bronze production. The gold mines of southeast Egypt produced a gold-silver ore with trace amounts of iron and nickel, which the Egyptians may have called djôm (𓈖𓄿𓏏𓏏).

Djôm is commonly translated as 'electrum' by Egyptologists, however, was recorded as a metal that the New Kingdom era Egyptians made weapons from, including chariots. The translation of djôm as 'electrum' is not new, the Classical era Greeks didn't know what djôm was either, and translated the word as electon (ἤλεκτρον), the name of a mythical metal that shone like the sun. As the early European Egyptologists knew little about Egyptian mineralogy, they adopted the term as 'electrum,' however, it is unlikely that the Egyptians would have built their weapons out of a soft metal, like gold, or a valuable metal, like gold, and no gold-silver alloy weapons have ever been found, suggesting that djôm was in fact the iron-nickel metal residue left over when the gold and silver was smelted from the gold ore.

The fact that the Egyptian General Siazara was stationed at a place called the Forge-of-the-Foreigners, implies the Egyptians were using something they had conquered from a group of foreigners to build the iron chariots he was reported to have had. The term Forge-of-the-Foreigners, is, unfortunately, not usually translated, but transliterated in most Bibles, and therefore the meaning of the name is lost. This is not a new practice, as the Greeks transliterated the name as Arisôth tôn ethnôn (Αρισωθ των εθνων), meaning: Arisoth of Nations. The Masoretic text contain charoshet hagGovyim (חֲרֹשֶׁת הַגּוֹיִם), which translates as 'The forge of the gentiles' or 'The forge of the foreigners,' however, this is generally transliterated as Harosheth Hagoyim, or partially translated as Harosheth of the Gentiles.

The Egyptians themselves are known to have produced smelted iron since at least the Old Kingdom era as a by-product of gold and bronze production, however, the quantities were very minimal, and the value of the iron produced was greater than the value of gold until the New Kingdom era.

Iron was used in Egypt in greater quantities during the Hyksos Dynasty, however, an iron industry never became established in Egypt under their rule, indicating they were using one or more forges in Canaan to produce their iron weaponry. One iron smelting site is known from the New Kingdom era, Site 200, in the Timna Valley, in Jordan, however, it is unclear if it was in use during the Hyksos Dynasty. The main reason that iron production was never established in Egypt under the Hyksos, was because the source of iron that would later be used in the Late Period was in the mountains of southern Egypt, near the gold mines, which the Hyksos never gained control over, however, there was likely also another reason.

Even after iron became the primary metal being used across the Middle East and the Mediterranean, between 1200 and 1000 BC, the Egyptians did not widely adopt it, instead, continuing to develop better forms of bronze that could compete with iron. This did not end until the

Empire of Kush conquered the Egyptians, and instituted wide-scale iron production between 744 and 656 BC.

By the time the Kushites conquered Egypt, Egypt was centuries behind the metallurgical technology of its neighbors. There is no obvious political or religious reason for Egypt having not adopted iron a thousand years earlier, implying an economic reason, likely an agreement between bronze working guilds that dated back thousands of years to the Old Kingdom or earlier. The Egyptians did not accept change easily, and it appears neither the Hyksos, who conquered them from Canaan nor the Libyans who later conquered them from the Sahara could convince them to implement iron production. Unlike the previous invaders, the Kushites did not depend on their conquest for economic stability as Kush provided all the food and iron they needed to rule their empire. Under the pressure of having to compete with Kushite metallurgists, the Egyptians finally acquiesced, and Egypt finally joined the iron age.

The Forge-of-the-Foreigners referred to in the Judges, was most likely a forge left over from the Hyksos dynasty, somewhere along the Kishion river, in northern Israel. The alliance between the renegade King Jabin and Egyptian General Siazara, which in the Septuagint's chronology seized control of Canaan in 1334 BC, a year when Egypt had three pharaohs: Smenkhkare,

Neferneferuaten, and Tutankhamen, implies that Siazara and his army did not accept any of the Pharaohs as legitimate. If Siazara's name was any indicator, he was a Ra worshiper, and as the worship of Ra had been banned by Akenaten, he likely saw the bond between the monarchy and the gods as having been severed, meaning the entire royal family would have been invalidated. This view could only have been validated by meeting Tutankhamen himself, as the boy was the product of generations of inbreeding, and suffered from several hereditary diseases. Even as a child, he could not walk without a cane. His young death, at 18 years of age, has been a matter of wide debate, with historians once having accused Ay of assassinating him. Based on the study of his remains, it appears he died of natural causes related to his genetic diseases.

According to Judges, an Israelite named Barak defeated Siazara and restored peace to Canaan in 1314 BC, when Deborah sang her song that referred to the sun as Aten, implying that the Israelites had remained loyal to the Egyptian monarchy throughout the insurrection of Jabin and Siazara. This would have been five years into the reign of Horemheb, when Egypt restored control over southern Canaan, however, did so without using the Egyptian military. The exact means that Horemheb used has traditionally been a mystery within Egyptology, however, the Book of Judges states it was the Israelites themselves that restored Egyptian control over the region, as Barak became the judge of Israel after defeating Siazara, and the land was peaceful for 40 years, until 1274 BC, which was the same year that Ramesses II marched his army north to attack the Nesite Empire according to Egyptologists.

The synchronizations between the Book of Judges and the records of Egypt are far too many to be overlooked or ignored. As almost all denominations of Christians and Jews agree that King Saul established his kingdom in 1037 BC, and the Septuagint's version of Judges includes 460 years of the land being ruled by Judges, or foreign kings, followed by an era of chaos when there was no king, the latest possible date the Exodus could have taken place was the 1500s BC, which supports the idea that the 10 plagues of Egypt were descriptions of the fallout and effects of the Minoan eruption which Egyptologists date to 1550 BC. According to Joshua, 42 years later the Israelites invaded Samaria, (northern modern Israel and the Palestinian West Bank) under the leadership of Joshua, which would have been 1508 BC. The plan was already laid out in the Book of Joshua to occupy the entire land of Canaan, yet just three years later, when Joshua was 85 years old, the Israelites stopped their campaign, after having only occupied the cities in Samaria, this would have been in 1505 BC.

The reason they stopped their invasion is not given, however, Egyptian records do explain it, as in the same year, 1505 BC, Pharaoh Thutmose I marched his army through Canaan to reconquer it for the Egyptian Empire. It had previously been under the control of the Hyksos Dynasty whose empire collapsed in the aftermath of the Minoan eruption. In 1550 BC, the Hyksos capital fell to the rival southern dynasty of Pharaoh Ahmose I, and the Hyksos retreated to their fortress of Sharuhen, near modern Gaza in the Palestinian Gaza Strip. This suggests the Hyksos maintained control over Canaan until Sharuhen fell to Ahmose I in 1540 BC. Ahmose I led an invasion of southern Canaan a few years later in an attempt to root out any remaining Hyksos. Egyptologists are not sure when this campaign was, placing it sometime between 1537 and 1527 BC. This campaign is not believed to have reached farther north than Byblos, in modern Lebanon, and did not result in any long-term political control over Canaan. Ahmose I's main goal seems to have been to destroy any remaining Hyksos in the region to ensure they did not try to recapture Egypt.

For decades after the conquest of Avaris, the new 18th Dynasty struggled to control Egypt, with numerous insurrections reported in the Nile Delta and Nubia, and does not appear to have tried to re-exert control over Canaan until Thutmose I's armies occupied the region in 1505 BC. Thutmose I marched his army all the way north to the Euphrates River in Syria, and reported all the peoples of Canaan surrendered to him without conflict, he then returned to Egypt and marched his army south to Nubia to suppress an insurrection there later that year. This means his army was only briefly in Canaan and did not have time to conquer any of the cities there, so either they did surrender without conflict, or, he lied. While the Book of Judges does not mention the Egyptian army passing through, this seems to have been redacted at a later point, as Joshua did stop his campaign in 1505 BC, and did not declare himself king, instead taking the subservient role of judge. Joshua's becoming a judge, means he ruled over a group of people but was under the authority of a king. The people were obviously the Israelites, and the king could only have been Thutmose I. This is an anticlimactic end to the tail of escape from Egypt and was likely redacted during the era of the two kingdoms when Egypt was again a foreign enemy.

According to Judges, Joshua judged the Israelites until he was 110 years old and then died in what would have been 1480 BC, following which Kushan Rishatayim ruled the Israelites. While the Hebrew term Kush (כּוּשׁ)

referred to the land of Kush, south of Egypt, whose people were known as the Kushi (כּוּשִׁי), Kushan (כושן) was a different term, which the Greeks did not recognize, and therefore transliterated it as Chousa (Χουσα). As the term referred to someone who was the king in the rivers of Aram (Syria), the origin of the word was almost certainly Kasium (𒀭𒍑𒈨), today translated as Kassite. The Kassites were the rulers of Babylonia in the late bronze age from some time in the 1500s BC, until 1155 BC, when they were conquered by the Elamites.

The Hebrew term rishatayim (רִשְׁעָתַיִם) is not proper Hebrew, Canaanite, or Aramaic, however, may be a the ancient Canaanite spelling of the name of king Paarshataar (𒆜𒄴𒂗𒀪𒌋𒄴), more commonly transliterated as Barattarna today, king of the Mitanni Empire circa 1485 BC. Barattarna is recorded as occupying northern Canaan during the reign of Hatshepsut by establishing a series of puppet states across the region, and gaining access to the Mediterranean Sea.

In circa 1479 BC, the Egyptian king Thutmose II died, and his former queen Hatshepsut seized the throne in the name of his two year old son Thutmose III. Hatshepsut was not the mother of Thutmose III, another wife Iset was, whom Hatshepsut married after officially changing her sex to male. After changing genders Hatshepsut declared himself to be Thutmose III's regent, although later assumed the role of king himself until his death, when Thutmose III inherited the throne. While Hatshepsut was a very unpopular king, his rule established the dominant architectural style of the New Kingdom.

The entire concept of a female king was rejected by many, with graffiti mocking King Hatshepsut's gender appearing in the archaeological record of the era. Most of Kush appears to have rejected Hatshepsut, and rebelled against his rule. After inheriting the throne in circa 1458 BC, Thutmose III attempted to erase Hatshepsut's rule from Egyptian records, claiming to have ruled continuously from the death of Thutmose II in circa 1479 BC. While her role as queen of Thutmose II was never erased, the era when Hatshepsut ruled Egypt was, and his era as king was not rediscovered until the 1800s.

It is clear that there was a rebellion against King Hatshepsut in Syria, backed by the Mitanni, and control of all territory north of Megiddo was lost, as the first thing Thutmose III did after assuming the throne was march north into Canaan, where he fought the battle of Megiddo against the rebelling Syrian kings, and their Mitanni allies. The Battle of Megiddo was the largest battle recorded in Egyptian records up until that time, with both the Egyptians and Canaanite rebels estimated to have fielded around 1,000 chariots and 10,000 infantry.

After defeating the Canaanites in the initial battle, the Egyptians plundered 924 chariots and 200 suits of armor. The Canaanite kings fell back to the fortified city of Kadesh, which the Egyptians then besieged for seven months. According to the records at Karnak, when the city surrendered the Egyptians captured 340 Canaanite and Mitanni princes, 2,041 mares, 191 foals, 6 stallions, 924 chariots, 200 suits of armor, 502 bows, 1,929 cattle, and 22,500 sheep.

Between 1458 and 1425 BC, Thutmose III fought a series of campaigns in Canaan, pushing Egyptian control north to the Euphrates River, and then crossed it into the Mitanni empire, where he plundered the country, which apparently had not rebuilt its defenses after the loss at Megiddo. After securing Canaan, Thutmose III marched his army south into Nubia, recapturing territory as far as the fourth cataract, all of which had been lost under the rule of Hatshepsut.

It is unclear why the author would have referred to Barattarna as a Kassite unless it was actually written at the time. The Mitanni rulers are often linked to the Kassites culturally, however, the peoples they ruled were not culturally similar. During the wars of Thutmose III in Canaan, the term Mitanni become common, however, earlier records simply called the land Naharin, meaning 'Rivers,' and called the people Hurrians. While the Hurrians were the primary population of the Mitanni Empire, the rulers were an unrelated group of Indo-Aryans, who spoke a language similar to Sanskrit, and worshiped the Vedic gods. They appear to have seized power over the Hurrians in the Khabur river region in the 1550s BC, from which they expanded in every direction until the Battle of Megiddo.

The Mitanni relationship with the Kassites is unclear, as the Kassites are not viewed as being Indo-Aryans, however, may have been Hurrians. The two cultures were close at the time, and it is plausible that the earliest Mitanni to arrive in the region were viewed as being Kassites by the Canaanites. Nevertheless, by 1457 BC the term would have already been anachronistic, as the term Mitanni would have replaced it, suggesting this verse was written between 1472 and 1457 BC.

In Judges, after the Kassite Barattarna was deposed, the land was peaceful for 40 years under Judge Othniel, which would have been between 1472 and 1432 BC. This era corresponds to the reign of the Kings Hatshepsut (1479-1458 BC) and Thutmose III (1458-1425 BC). Thutmose III fought 17 campaigns in northern Canaan during the era, however, southern Canaan appears to have been peaceful throughout most of the era under the protection of the Egyptian army. During Thutmoses' campaign against the rebelling cities of Megiddo and Kadesh in his first year on the throne, Habiru (𒄩 𒌋 𒁺) archers were recorded as escorting Thutmose III and his army through the Aruna mountain pass (Wadi Ara), supporting the claims that the ancestors of the Hebrews were loyal to Egypt at the time.

According to Judges, this era of peace in southern Canaan ended in 1432 BC when Eglon the king of Moab conquered the Israelites east of the Jordan River. These Israelites appear to have never been under Egyptian governance, and the war east of the Jordan appears to have been separate from, yet inspired by the general insurrection against Egypt in northern Canaan. This conquest of the eastern Israelites by Eglon the Moabite is referred to at the end of Joshua, right after the death of Joshua, implying the book of Joshua originated with the eastern tribes, who lived in peace between 1480 and 1432 BC. After 18 years of domination by the Moabites, King Eglon was killed by an Israelite named Ehud, which began a period of 80 years of peace, during which Eglon and then Shamgar were the Judges of Israel. This time span would have been 1414 to 1334 BC, ending when the Egyptian monarchical power collapsed at the end of the Amarna period, and King Jabin of Hazor and General Siazara rebelled.

After Jabin and Siazara were defeated the land had another peaceful era of forty years under Judge Barak, who had defeated Siazara. Barak's wife was the prophet Deborah, to whom the Song of Deborah is attributed. The Song of Deborah, which is chapter 5 of Judges, is generally considered by scholars to be the oldest piece of Israelite literature to survive more or less intact to the present. While Barak was the leader who defeated the army of Siazara, it was Jael, the wife of Eber the blacksmith who killed Siazara after taking him to her bedchamber and then driving a stake through his temple.

The significance of the blacksmiths in Judges is often also overlooked, as the word blacksmith is generally transliterated as Kenite, implying a tribe. This is not a new practice, as the Greeks did the same thing when they translated the Septuagint, transliterating the Hebrew word for blacksmith: keini (קֵינִי) as Cinaeou (Κιναιου). The significance of the metal-smiths, especially iron-smiths, which is what the word keini likely meant in Judges, was lost in the millennium between the age of Deborah, and the age of the Ptolemies, likely because by then metallurgy was universal, including iron-working. These 'Kenites' were so significant at the time, that even Moses appears to have married his daughter to one, named Jobab. This story has been lost, however, the reference to Jobab the 'groom of Moses' has survived in both the Septuagint and Masoretic Text.

The connection between Siazara's army being based at the Forge-of-the-Foreigners, and him being killed by the wife of a blacksmith cannot be ignored. The fact that he was listed as commanding 900 iron war-chariots also cannot be overlooked, as that would have been a major division within the Egyptian army at the time, and likely the entire Egyptian army stationed in Canaan.

After the defeat of Siazara and Jabin, Judges states that the land was peaceful for 40 years under Judge Barak, which would have been between 1314 and 1274 BC. This era of peace ended when the Midianites, Amalekites, and the 'sons of the east' conquered the Israelites in 1274 BC. 1274 BC is also the year that Egyptologists claim that Pharaoh Ramesses II launched his disastrous First Syrian Campaign. The Egyptian army was soundly defeated by the Nesites, allowing nomadic groups like the Amalakites and Midianites to plunder Canaan as described in the Book of Judges.

The 'sons of the East' in the Book of Judges are likely none other than the Nesites, commonly misidentified as Hittites, as they came from the region north of the Euphrates, which while being geographic nonsense in the modern mindset, was considered to be the east by the ancient Canaanites, as one had to head north to the Euphrates before heading east into Mesopotamia. It's likely the Israelites did not know where exactly the

Nesites were from and assumed it was the east in Mesopotamia, like the Babylonians and Assyrians.

According to Judges, the Midianites ruled Israel for 7 years, between 1274 and 1267 BC, however, it is not clear if these Israelites were east or west of the Jordan, and therefore, they may not have been the Israelites in Egyptian-ruled Canaan. Ramesses II's Second Syrian Campaign, in 1273 BC was equally disastrous, and his army was defeated again, although did make it to the outskirts of Kadesh. His Third Syrian Campaign, in 1271 BC, was focused on reconsolidating Egyptian authority outside of Nesite-controlled areas, and he marched his army from city to city in Canaan demanding tribute. Cities that offered tribute were considered loyal to Egypt, and left alone, while those that refused were sacked. Edom, Seir, Moab, Jerusalem, Jericho, Heshbon, and Damascus are all listed as cities or lands that were visited by the army, although it is not clear which were loyal and which were sacked.

In 1270 and 1267 BC, Ramesses II's armies marched against Kadesh again and managed to drive the Nesites from the region. The Book of Judges claims that the Shechemite leader Abimelech defeated the Midianites and their Amakaite and Nesite (sons of the East) allies in 1267 BC, and became the King of Israel, however, his kingdom appears to have been rejected by most

Israelites, and he was described in the Book of Judges as a real bastard, the son of a prostitute. His kingdom only lasted 3 years, until 1264 BC, when the other Israelites under the leadership of Judge Tola overthrew him.

There were 23 peaceful years under Judge Tola, followed by 22 under Judge Jair, which would have been between 1264 and 1219 BC. During this era, King Ramesses was focused on defending Egypt from a naval power called the 'Sea Peoples' by Egyptologists. It is unclear where they were based, however, Sardinia and Greece are the two dominant theories. Ramesses signed a peace treaty with the Nesite King Hattusili III in 1258 BC, and Canaan does appear to have been peaceful throughout the era of Judges Tola and Jair. During that era, Ramesses built a series of forts along the Mediterranean coast of modern Egypt, for the first time in recorded history attempting to protect the desert-routes from the invasions of these Sea Peoples.

This peaceful era in southern Canaan ended abruptly in 1219 BC according to Judges, when the Pelesets and Ammonites seized control of the region. Egyptian records depict this as a time of great unrest, as the war with the Sea Peoples was still going on, and Ramesses II died in 1213 BC, after being Pharaoh for 66 years. In 1208 and 1207 BC, the Sea People launched a major invasion of Egypt, and control of the Nile Delta was briefly lost. Pharaoh Merneptah (1213-1203 BC) appears to have negotiated an agreement with the Sea Peoples in 1207 BC which allowed them to settle in Canaan if they returned the Nile Delta, and the following year, 1206 BC, Canaanite towns and tribes were listed in open revolt against Egyptian authority, with the list of rebels including Gaza, Ashkelon, Yenoam, Israel, and the Arameans.

It is unclear what level of authority the Egyptian New Kingdom exerted over Canaan after 1206 BC, however, the Book of Judges reports that Judge Jephthah defeated the Moabites in 1201 BC, and judged the Israelites for 6 years. He was followed by the judges Ibzan, Elon, and Abdon, who judged the Israelites until 1170 BC when the Pelesets (also called Philistines or Palestinians) seized control of southern Canaan.

This occupation of southern Canaan by the Pelesets, recorded in Judges, is also recorded by the Egyptians, carved into the walls of the mortuary temple of Pharaoh Ramesses III at Medinet Habu. According to the Egyptian records from the era, several groups of Sea Peoples attacked Egypt in waves between 1179 and 1174 BC, including groups known as the Peleset, Denyen, Shardana. Peleset is the Egyptian name for the Pelesets, while the Denyen are believed to have been the Danoi tribe of ancient Greece, and the Shardana were the

Egyptians' main antagonists of the previous century, generally thought to have been Sardinians.

These attacks during the reign of Ramesses III were the worst Egypt had seen, with allied over land attacks by the Meshwesh tribes of Libya, and the Tjekker, a group of Sea Peoples that had occupied and fortified the town of Dor, on the northern coast of modern Israel a few decades earlier. While Ramesses III's records report that he graciously allowed the Pelesets to live in southern Canaan after he defeated them, it appears that all his forces could do was defend the Nile Delta, and the Pelesets captured Egypt's northern-most territory.

Based on the records in Judges, the Israelites recognized the authority of the Pelests in 1170 BC, four years after their last battle against Egypt. This appears to have been the end of the New Kingdom's authority in southern Canaan, however, after 40 years of Peleset rule, Samson rose as a Judge of Israel under Peleset rule. He was described as judging Israel for 20 years during the Peleset era, before leading a failed revolt against them and being captured by his favorite prostitute. After Samson's heroic suicide, the Book of Judges indicates that his father Manoah judged Israel for another 20 years, before the era of chaos, when there was no king.

This era of chaos in Canaan would have begun in 1090 BC, shortly before the same thing happened in Egypt in 1077 BC. Egyptologists call this the Third Intermediate Period, as there are few records from the era. In Greece, where civilization collapsed at approximately the same time, it would later be called the Dark Age, which then inspired the name of the Dark Age that followed the collapse of the Roman Empire in Western Europe. During this Dark Age of ancient Canaan, the book of Judges records that there was no king, however, a lot did happen during this era implying it lasted several decades. During this era, the Danites conquered Laish and renamed it Dan, and the Benjamite genocide took place.

The Danites had been described as living on boats until this era, which some modern historians have taken as evidence that they were new arrivals in Canaan, likely related to the Danoi tribe of Greece. This is most likely not correct, as the name Dan appears in many ancient Canaanite texts, and appears to have been common in ancient Canaan.

The Benjaminite genocide was a strange story set in this era as well and likely tied to the downfall of Lord Lahem, the fertility god of ancient Canaan that Bethlehem was named after. The story involved the Benjaminites in the town of Gibeah attempting to gang-rape a young man who had stopped there for the night. He had been taken in by an old man that lived in the city, and when the men of the city demanded the old man hand over the young man so they could rape him, the old man gave them his daughter and the young man's concubine instead, who were raped to death. When the other Israelite tribes heard of this event, they virtually wiped out the Benjaminites. It is a strange story to have been simply made up and added to the historical narrative of Judges, which up until this dark age had been fairly consistent with Egyptian records of their rule of Canaan, indicating the story was likely based on something that had happened.

The Benjaminite genocide took a number of years and resulted in most of the tribe being destroyed. During the genocide the other tribes vowed to not allow Benjaminites to marry their daughters, however, by the end, the other tribes took pity on them, and allowed their daughters to be abducted by Benjaminites to become their wives. While every aspect of the story is odd, the strangest aspect of the story is the part not found in Judges, but in 1st Kingdoms (Masoretic Samuel), the fact that King Saul was a Benjaminite. As this genocide took place sometime between 1090 and 1037 BC, it is strange that a Benjaminite could have become king in

1037 BC. A lot of this story has been lost in the past 3000 years.

The story of the rape itself appears to have simply been a catalyst for the Benjaminite genocide, as the murder of an entire tribe seems excessive punishment for any crime committed by a few members of the tribe. The genocide of Benjamin was likely related to the fall of the Egyptian Empire, as the tribe was the most Egyptianized of the Israelite tribes. Even their name was Egyptian: Pen-Amen (𓊪𓏌𓇋𓏌𓏏, Middle Egyptian transliteration pån-jômån), which meant Son of Amen. Amen (𓇋𓏠𓈖), also transliterated into English as Amun or Amon, was the father god of the Theban triad, and supreme god of Egypt throughout the New Kingdom era, other than during the brief Amarna Period. The Egyptian tale, the Voyage of Wenamen, set during the same era as King Saul, described the journey of a Theban priest of Amen's travels in Canaan, and his shock that everyone in Canaan had lost respect for Amen after the Egyptian Empire had collapsed.

The Book of Judges itself is very old, and the Song of Deborah may be the oldest surviving piece of Israelite literature, as it uses some of the most archaic forms of Canaanite in the Masoretic Text. Within the book of Judges, the spoken dialect was part of the division between the Israelites during the battle between the

Gileadites from east of the Jordan, and the Ephraimites from west of the Jordan. The spelling of šblt (שבלת) in the Masoretic Text is not the Hebrew spelling of šybwlt (שיבולת), but the older Canaanite spelling, recorded as šblt (𐎌𐎁𐎍𐎚) in Ugaritic Canaanite, and šblt (𐤔𐤁𐤋𐤕) in Phoenician Canaanite.

This older Canaanite spelling developed into the Hebrew spelling during the Persian era, under the influence of Imperial Aramaic. The older Akkadian cuneiform term was šubulta (𒅇𒀸𒁺𒋫), indicating that the division among the Israelites was already between those speaking Canaanite versus Aramaic. Arameans appeared in Mesopotamian records centuries earlier than the Habirus, and the two cultures were generally described as inhabiting the same regions, although the Arameans were more urban, and the Habirus were more nomadic.

There is evidence that the book was either assembled or redacted in the Kingdom of Samaria, as the book includes the name of the Canaanite sun-god Shemesh, whose worship was later banned in Judah by King Josiah in circa 625 BC. The region of the book also generally corresponds with the territory of the northern kingdom, both the region that had once been under Egyptian authority west of the Jordan and the region east of the Jordan which had generally been independent of Egypt. Conversely, the Aramaic book of Judges which was used as a source text by the Greeks appears to have been translated into Aramaic during the Persian era, as the Greek translation includes Persian loanwords the Greeks would not have used, such as satrap, the title of Persian governors.

Judges is a continuation of the story found in Joshua, but not a seamless one, as Joshua includes the Moabites occupying Samaria after the death of Joshua, which skips past 48 years of history recorded in Judges. This gap in Joshua reflects the fact that none of that 48 years of history affected the eastern Israelites who were outside the sphere of Egypt. This shows that the two books had different origins, Joshua from the eastern Israelites, and Judges from the western Israelites.

The two books were likely united as part of a historical narrative along with Deuteronomy in the Kingdom of Samaria between 930 and 720 BC. As Deuteronomy is a collection of amendments to the laws found in Exodus that generally repeats the amendments and stories of Leviticus and Numbers, it is likely it was composed in Samaria to serve the same function as Leviticus-Numbers would later serve in Judah. Deuteronomy and Joshua flow together seamlessly, implying that Joshua was once a part of Deuteronomy, however, Judges does not flow seamlessly from Joshua and is composed in an older dialect, implying the book was already very old by the time Deuteronomy-Joshua was organized into its pre-Hasmonean state by the Aaronite priesthood of Samaria.

The presence of the name Aten in the Song of Deborah proves that at least Chapter 5 dates back to the time it describes, the late-1300s BC. Only a few fragments of Judges have survived among the Dead Sea Scrolls, and all date to the Herodian Dynasty or later, meaning they all date to after the Hasmonean redaction of circa 140 BC. If some of the songs and stories found in the book of Judges were written in the 1300s BC, they could not have been written in the Phoenician script that emerged in the 1100s BC, suggesting an older script was used.

The Ugaritic script was being used in northern Canaan at the time, however, there is no evidence of it being used in southern or central Canaan. At the time, the Egyptian court was corresponding with the governors and judges throughout Canaan using the Akkadian cuneiform script, suggesting that was the script used, however, no clear evidence exists to support any of Judges being written in cuneiform, unlike Exodus and Joshua, which each include Akkadian loanwords. Nevertheless, there are terms related to Egypt that suggest a cuneiform precursor to the Phoenician version of Judges. The presence of the 'unknown' terms Aten and Meroz in the song of Deborah proves it must have been written in some script, and the spelling of the terms prh nôrk (פרה נערך), and prôwt (פרעות) in the Masoretic text supports this as having been in cuneiform.

Both prh nôrk (פרה נערך) and prôwt (פרעות) are also considered 'unknown' terms, resulting in some strange translations. The translators at the Library of Alexandria translated the term as 'Phara the child (or servant)' (Φαρα το παιδαριον), while the Hebrew translates as 'carrying-boy,' or 'cow-servant,' or possibly even 'cowboy.' Based on the context, this strange sentence appears to be a reference to an Egyptian overseer stationed by Pharaoh among the Tribe of Manasseh.

The Phoenician spelling of 'pharaoh' was prôh (𐤐𐤓𐤄), while the Aramaic spelling was prôwn (פרעון), neither of which is an exact match for the transliterated words prh (פרה) and phara (Φαρα), indicating that neither the Paleo-Hebrew nor Aramaic texts included the word 'pharaoh' but a similar sounding word. This indicates that the word, along with the Song of Deborah, was transliterated from another script, likely Akkadian Cuneiform or Egyptian.

The Akkadian Cuneiform spelling of 'pharaoh' was pirôû (𒉿𒀀𒌋) during the late Bronze Age, which would have been pronounced the same as the Masoretic word, while the Egyptian spelling was per-ôå (𒉺), which would have been pronounced slightly differently, supporting the Song of Deborah having been written in cuneiform.

Fragments of the book of Ruth have been found among the dead sea scrolls, however, only in the Assyrian script of the Hasmonean Dynasty, and dated to between 140 and 37 BC. Like Judges, the terms used in denoting the gods differ, with the Septuagint using the terms lord God (κυριω Θεω) or lord (κύριος), and the Masoretic Text using the names Yehvah (יְהוָה) and Yhvah (יהוָה).

The Masoretic Book of Ruth also includes a reference to the god Šdy (שדי), who was described as having 'dealt very bitterly' with Naomi when she was in Moab. In the Septuagint, the name was translated as ikanós (ικανοσ), meaning 'capable,' which indicates that the word Šdy (𐤔𐤃𐤉) was not in the Aramaic text the Greeks translated, however, a similar name was. Shaddai was in several of the books that ended up in both the Septuagint and the Masoretic Text, and in other books was translated into Greek as 'omnipotent' (παντοκρατοροσ) or transliterated directly in Greek as Saddai (Σαδδαι). This indicates that the god that dealt bitterly with Naomi was the Moabite god Shaddayin.

Šdyn (𐤔𐤃𐤉𐤍), generally anglicized as Shaddayin, was a Moabite god in the 800s BC, as evidenced by the Deir Alla Inscription (or KAI 312), which was found during an excavation at Deir 'Alla, Jordan, and described Balaam as the prophet of the Elohin and Shaddayin, believed to be Moabite translations of 'Elohim' and 'Shaddai.' In the Book of Ruth, Šdy is placed in opposition to the Lord God of Israel, which implies the name was left in the Judahite version of Ruth after the Hasmonean redaction as it was viewed as a reference to the Moabite god, who 'dealt very bitterly' with Naomi when she was in Moab.

The Greek and Hebrew translations often differ in regards to the name or title Shaddai, suggesting that the Aramaic and Canaanite (Judahite or Samaritan) source texts they worked from differed in regards to this word. The term was omitted throughout Cosmic Genesis, suggesting that when the word was first encountered the Greeks did not know how to interpret it. It is equally possible that it was the Aramaic translator who had omitted it, however, it was almost certainly in the Canaanite version the translator worked from, as it is used consistently in the rest of Genesis, and is mentioned again when Moses god's name Ān is introduced in the Septuagint's Exodus. The cause of the confusion over the term Shaddai, is likely due to the difference between the meaning of the word in Canaanite versus Aramaic.

In Akkadian cuneiform, which was adopted as the written script by many cultures, the term was [deity]Šēdu (✳𐎁), however, it referred to a 'protective spirit' or 'lesser god.' In the later Aramaic language, the word became šydå (𐎌𐎊𐎄), meaning 'demon' in the classical sense, as a type of muse or nymph. Whereas in Canaanite, šd (𐎌𐎄) took on a different meaning, generally interpreted as 'powerful' by the Early Classical Era, which is likely where the Greeks ultimately derived the term 'omnipotent' (παντοκράτοροσ), which was used later in the Septuagint where the Masoretic Text generally uses the term Shaddai.

This alternate interpretation of the šd (𐎌𐎄) in Canaanite is likely due to the Egyptian New Kingdom era rule over Canaan, when Shed (𓅱𓂧𓈙, transliteration: šd), was worshiped in the region. Shed, who was often referred to as 'the savior,' was virtually identical to the earlier Canaanite god Resheph who was largely suppressed after the fall of the Hyksos dynasty. In the Masoretic Book of Job, Eliphaz referred to humanity as the 'sons of Resheph' (בני-רשף) instead of the 'sons of Adam,' and then refers god as šdy (שדי). This usage is consistent throughout Masoretic Job, indicating that at some point the name Resheph was updated to Shaddai, likely during the New Kingdom era, when Resheph worship was suppressed due to his associated with the

earlier Hyksos dynasty. During the early New Kingdoms era, holy texts about Resheph would have been
updated to Shed (𓈙𓂧𓀭), which would have been
transliterated into Canaanite using the Akkadian Cuneiform script in the late New Kingdom era as ^{deity}Šēdu
(✳𒁹), before being translated into Canaanite using the
Phoenician script in the early iron age as šdy (𐤔𐤃𐤉),
resulting in the confusing 'god of demons' (𐡔𐡃𐡉) in
Aramaic. In this particular verse, 'capable' (ικανοσ)
appears to be a translation of a word similar to šdy (שׁדי),
but not actually šdy, or 'omnipotent' (παντοκράτοροσ)
would have been used, as in other books of the Septuagint, and therefore the Moabite version of the name,
Shaddayin, is used in this translation.

The Septuagint and Masoretic Text have different
names for Naomi's husband. He is called Abimelech
(αβιμελεχ) in the Codex Vaticanus, but Elimelech
(אֱלִימֶלֶךְ) in the Masoretic Text. It is not clear why the
Hasmoneans would have changed the name of this minor
character, however, it may have been to disassociate
King David from the first King of Israel, King Abimelech, who led an insurrection against Egypt and
declared himself king in 1267 BC. Other than the name
and the fact that both were Ephriamites, the two Abimelechs seem to have nothing in common. King Abimelech was the son of Gideon in the Book of Judges, who

was so unpopular the Israelites overthrew him and restored the judges after 3 years, in 1264 BC, following which he was killed.

The book of Ruth appears to be part of a Samaritan story designed to splice the Moabites into the royal genealogy. The Book of Deuteronomy, which was likely written in Samaria, uses Moabite names of locations instead of Judahite names, indicating that a Moabite priesthood was active in Samaria before the kingdom fell to the Assyrians.

The Book of Judges refers to King Abimelech as the bastard son of Gideon by a prostitute, which speaks volumes about his memory, however, he was an Ephraimite, as was the Abimelech in the Book of Ruth, indicating that he could not have been viewed that badly a century after his death, when Ruth's father in law would have been born. Ruth, the step-daughter of Abimelech in the Book of Ruth, ultimately became an ancestor of King David, meaning it is possible that some Israelites were connecting the two Abimelechs in the Second Temple era, claiming that David was a descendant of King Abimelech.

The setting of the Ruth is the lands of Judah and Moab in the early 1000s BC, when the Book of Judges claimed there was no king. The last judge under the

Pelesets in the books of Judges was Samson's father Manoah, who ruled until 1090 BC when the Peleset Kingdom apparently collapsed. This was just over a decade before the collapse of the Egyptian New Kingdom in 1077 BC, which began the Third Intermediate Period, when Egyptian records became sparse. This collapse of civilization in Canaan and Egypt was mirrored by collapses across the Mediterranean, sparking what the Greeks would later call the Dark Age. This Dark Age is not in doubt, however, is poorly understood due to the sparse records from the era. The story would have taken place around the same era as the Benjaminite genocide in the Book of Judges, which is likely the reason the book of Ruth was placed directly behind the book of Judges in the Septuagint.

It is not clear when the Book of Ruth was written, however, it is not generally considered to date back to the era it is set in. Based on the connection between the Book of Ruth and King David, it seems likely that the book was written no earlier than the era of King David, however, the book is generally dated to the time of Ezra the Scribe circa 350 BC. It is generally interpreted as an attempt to bridge the older books of Joshua and Judges with the newer books of the Kingdoms (Masoretic Samuel and Kings), which are generally accepted as having been compiled during the time of Ezra the scribe.

While the Hasmoneans may have tried to court Rome and the rebels in Phrygia and Assyria, there is little evidence that anyone other than the Assyrians was interested in allying with them. A series of wars including both Julius Caesar's campaigns, and a Parthian invasion led to the weakening of the Hasmonean dynasty, and in 37 AD, the Roman Senate appointed Herod the Great as King of the Jews. Herod's rule wasn't particularly popular, as he allowed the Romans to establish themselves within Judea, however, he did expand Judea, reintegrating the Greek and Samaritan cities, and annexing Galilee and Edom. When he died, his kingdom was divided between four successors, a situation that ended in 66 AD when the Romans conquered the region. An uprising in 120 AD led to the Jews being exiled from Judea, and the region became a Greco-Roman colony. In the wake of the Jews, the Samaritans rose in numbers, along with the Christians once Christianity was legalized. Between 529 and 555 AD, the Samaritans revolted and were effectively annihilated, by Constantinople the Byzantine capital.

The modern Samaritan religion is similar to Judaism, in that they have versions of the Torah and the book of Joshua, however, they do not trace their ancestry to ancient Judah, but rather to ancient Samaria also called the Northern Kingdom of Israel. According to the Samaritans, they were the original Israelites, and the Temple of the Lord was not Solomon's Temple in Jerusalem, but rather a Temple of Mount Gerizim, in Samaria. These other Israelites also contributed to the creation of the Septuagint, as the Book of Tobit, was the story of a Samaritan that had been taken to Nineveh, the capital of the Assyrian Empire after the Kingdom of Israel was conquered by the Assyrians. This book and several others were not considered important to Simon the Zealot, and not translated into Hebrew.

Outside of Judea, the Septuagint was the dominant form of Israelite scriptures across the Greek-speaking world, which at the beginning of the Christian era extended from the Roman Empire in the west, to the Indo-Greek Kingdom in the east. Judean traders had established small colonies along the trade routes of the Red Sea and the Indian Ocean, reaching as far south as Eritrea, and as far east as southern India, and these Judeans spoke Aramaic and Greek and used the Septuagint. The earliest Christians used the Septuagint exclusively, as far as the Israelite scriptures were concerned, and as a result, it is impossible to even understand the chronology of the world they described unless using the Septuagint. It is unclear why the Septuagint, Masoretic Text, and Samaritan Asatir each contain a different chronology of the world. Adding the Book of Jubilees, and various variations of the Torah found within the Dead Sea Scrolls, there are no less than six ancient Israelite chronologies.

The Septuagint's Genesis includes an additional millennium of human history that was dropped from the Proto-Masoretic Texts in order to align the creation of the world with the beginning of the age of El, when the constellation Taurus became the marker of the northern vernal equinox, in 3760 BC. The Bull El was the dominant God of the Canaanite pantheon until circa 1700 BC, when Attar the Goat (Aries) and Yam the Sea-Monster (Cetus) fought for domination of the world beneath the sky, ultimately both being replaced by the god of thunder Ba'al Hadad, in the Canaanite Ba'al Cycle. Traditional Jewish interpretations of the timeline within the Masoretic Text, is further hampered by the so-called 'missing years' of Rabbinical Time, in which hundreds of years of the Persian Empire are skipped over in order to make the timeline fit into the era since 3760 BC, a problem Christian chronologists have never had as Christianity developed after the astrology of Babylonian-era Judaism had been forgotten.

The earliest Christian Bibles all used the Septuagint, however, by the 4th century some Christian scholars were debating whether they should retranslate the Old Testament from the version the Jews were using, and some even suggested using the Samaritan version. Both suggestions were generally dismissed as heretical, as Jesus and the Apostles had quoted from the Septuagint, even though they had access to the Hebrew version then in use. This argument held in the west until the Middle Ages, when Catholic Bibles switched to the Masoretic Text. In the east, Orthodox Bibles continued to use the Septuagint, as they do today. To the south, the Ethiopian Tewahedo Church continued to use the Septuagint, and across Asia, the Thomas Christians and Nestorians continued to use the Septuagint. Only in Western Europe were the later Masoretic Text adopted, abandoning the more ancient Septuagint, on the assumption that the Jews had copied their texts more faithfully than the Greeks had translated them. This assumption was carried forward into the Protestant Churches that broke off from the Catholic Church, and therefore almost all Protestant Bibles use the Masoretic Text for the basis of the Old Testament.

Unfortunately, this means that the earliest Christian writings are generally confusing and ignored by Protestants and Catholics. The earliest Christians of the first and second centuries quoted books that are no longer in the Bible, and as such, their writings are not always understood. Septuagint: Judges and Ruth is part of a series of 21st century translations aimed at correcting this problem.

One of the problems with academic translations of the Septuagint, is the use of unfamiliar names or terms, as the Septuagint was written in Greek, and therefore many names are unrecognizable to modern readers who are used to Hebrew-derived names. This project uses the more commonly understood Hebrew-derived names instead of their Greek translations, such as Canaan instead of Chanaan, and Melchizedek instead of Melchisedec. Common modern names are also used instead of either Greek or Hebrew terms when geographical locations are known, such as the archaeological name Uruk instead of the Greek Orech, or the Hebrew Erech, and the archaeological term Sumer instead of Shinar or Senar. While this could be argued as not being a correct academic procedure, it does fulfill the goal of making the translation easy to read and understand.

Judges: Chapter 1

After the death of Joshua, the Israelites asked the Lord,[1] "Who will go up for us first against the Canaanites, to fight against them?"

The Lord answered, "Judah will go up. Watch, I have delivered the land into his hand."

Judah said to his brother Simeon, "Come up with me into my allotted territory and let us ally ourselves against the Canaanites, and I also will go with you into your allotted territory," and Simeon went with him. Judah went up, and the Lord delivered the Canaanite and the Perizzite into their hands, and they slaughtered ten thousand men in Bezek.[2] They defeated the Lord of Bezek[3] in Bezek and fought against him, and they attacked the Canaanites and the Perizzites. The Lord of Bezek fled, and they chased after him, and caught him, and cut off his thumbs and his big toes.

The Lord of Bezek said, "Seventy kings collected their food from my table after I cut their thumbs and their big toes off. As I have done, God has repaid me."

They brought him to Jerusalem, and he died there.

The children of Judah attacked Jerusalem and plundered it, and slaughtered by the edge of the sword, and burnt the city with fire. Afterward, the children of

Judah went down to fight with the Canaanites living in the hill country, and the Negev, and the plain country.

Judah went to the Canaanites who lived in Hebron and Hebron came out against him. (Previously, Hebron was called the village of Arbaseifer.) They slaughtered Sheshai, Ahiman, and Tamlai, the descendants of Anaks.

They went up from there to the inhabitants of Debir. (Debir was previously called the village of Seifer [City of Letters.])[5]

Caleb said, "Whoever will attack the village of Seifer, and will capture it first, I will give him my daughter Acsah as a wife."

Othniel the younger son of Kenez the brother of Caleb captured it, and Caleb gave him his daughter Acsah as a wife. It happened as she went in, that Othniel urged her to ask for a field from her father, and she whined and cried from her donkey, "You have sent me out into a southern land."

Caleb asked her, "What is your request?"

Acsah answered him, "Give me a blessing, I beg of you, for you have sent me out to a southern land, and you will give me the prize of water," and Caleb gave her according to her heart the prize of the upper springs and the low springs.

The children of Jobab the blacksmith[6] the son-in-law of Moses went up from the city of palm-trees[7] with the children of Judah, to the wilderness that is to the south of Judah, which is at the descent of Arad, and they lived with the people. Judah went with Simeon his brother and slaughtered the Canaanites that inhabited Zephath, and they completely destroyed them, and they called the name of the city Anathema.[8] But Judah did not inherit Gaza and her coast, or Ashkelon and her coast, or Ekron and her coast, or Ashdod and the lands around it. The Lord was with Judah, and he inherited the mountain, as they were not able to destroy the inhabitants of the valley, for Rechab[9] prevented them. They gave Hebron to Caleb, as Moses said, and there he inherited the three cities of the children of Anaks. But the Benjaminites did not take the inheritance of the Jebusites who lived in Jerusalem, and the Jebusites lived with the Benjaminites in Jerusalem until this day.

The sons of Joseph also went up to the Temple of El[10] and the Lord was with them. They camped and surveyed the Temple of El (the name of the town was Luz[11] then). The spies looked and saw a man go out of the city, and they captured him, and said, "Show us the way into the city, and we will deal mercifully with you."

He showed them the way into the city, and they slaughtered the city with the edge of the sword, but they let the man and his family go. The man went into the land of the Cypriots,[12] and built a city there called Luz,[13] and this is its name until this day.

Manasseh did not drive out the inhabitants of the House of She'an[14] (which is Scythopolis), or her towns and her suburbs, nor Ti'inik[15] and her towns, nor the inhabitants of Dor[16] and her suburbs and towns, or the inhabitants of Balak[17] and her suburbs and her towns, or the inhabitants of Megiddo[18] and her suburbs and towns, or the inhabitants of Belameh[19] and her suburbs and towns. The Canaanites began to live in this land. It happened when Israel was strong, that he made the Canaanites tributary, but did not completely drive them out.

Ephraim did not drive out the Canaanites that lived in Gezer, and the Canaanites lived among them in Gezer and became tributary.

Zebulun did not drive out the inhabitants of Kitron, nor the inhabitants of Domana,[20] and the Canaanites lived among them and became tributary to them.

Asher did not drive out the inhabitants of Acco who became tributary to him, or the inhabitants of Dor,[21] Sidon,[22] Ahlab,[23] Achazib,[24] Helbah, Nai,[25] or Ereo.[26]

Asher lived among the Canaanites who inhabited the land, for they could not drive them out.

Naphtali did not drive out the inhabitants of House of Shemesh,[27] or the inhabitants of House of Anat,[28] and Naphtali lived among the Canaanites who inhabited the land, but the inhabitants of House of Shemesh and House of Anat became tributary to them.

The Amorites drove out the children of Dan into the mountains, and they did not allow them to come down into the valley. The Amorites began to live in the clay mountains,[29] where there are bears and foxes, in Myrsinoni[30] and Sha'alvim.[31] The hand of the house of Joseph was heavy on the Amorites, and they became tributary to them. The border of the Amorites was from the ascent of Akrabbim,[32] from the Petra[33] and upwards.

Judges: Chapter 1 Notes

1 Codex Vaticanus: tou cyriou (ΤΟΥΚΥΡΙΟΥ). Translation: the Lord

- Codex Alexandrinus: en cyriô (ЄΝΚΥΡΙѠ). Translation: of Lord

- Aleppo Codex: byhwh (בִּיהוּה). Translation: in (or with, while, among, on) Yhwh

- Leningrad Codex: baYhvah (בַּיהֹוָה). Translation: in (or with, while, among, on) Yhvah

- Targum Jerusalem: daYeyah (דְּיֵיָ). Translation: of (or from) Yahw

This chapter does not survive among the Dead Sea Scrolls, however, the name Yhwh does survive in later sections of Judges that have survived among the Dead Sea Scrolls.

- Dead Sea Scroll 4QJudg^a: Yhwh (יהוה)

- Dead Sea Scroll 4QJudg^b: Yhwh (יהוה)

The Septuagint's version of the Judges was translated before 200 BC, as it was carried south by the Beta Israel community, who left Egypt for Kush (modern Sudan) during the Jewish Rebellion against the Ptolemys in 200 BC. This means it predates the Hasmonean redaction and contains the term Lord (Κύριος) instead of Iaw (Ιαω), which, if correctly translated from the Aramaic source texts, would have read ådny (אדני). The Greeks are believed to have transliterated Yhw (יהו), the Aramaic version of the name Yhvah/Yehvah, as Iaô (Ιαω) in the Book of Leviticus, published circa 250 BC, as evidenced by the Dead Sea Scroll Septuagint fragment 4QpapLXXLev[b], which dates from Hasmonean era Judea. 4QpapLXXLev[b] could be interpreted as a Hasmonean redaction of the Septuagint, however, Leviticus appears to have been written during the rule of King Josiah, and his God was Yahw, supporting the existence of Yahw in the Book of Leviticus. The Aramaic sections of Masoretic Daniel that were not translated into Hebrew maintain the term adonai ha'elohim (אֲדֹנָי֙ הָאֱלֹהִ֔ים), meaning the 'Lord the gods' where the Septuagint has 'Lord the god' (Κύριον τὸν θεὸν), however, the Hebrew sections have Yehvah elohim (יְהוָ֥ה אֱלֹהִ֖ים) where the Septuagint has 'Lord the god,' suggesting the Greek more accurately reflects the Aramaic source texts than the Hebrew translation. According to the Talmud, this was to repair the damage King Manasseh had done 600 years earlier when he removed the name Yehvah from the Israelite Texts, however, no evidence has survived from the era of Manasseh or earlier that proves the name was originally in the text, suggesting it was an attempt by the first Hasmonean High-Priest/King Simon the Zealot to create a national Judean religion with a god having a name similar to the Roman god Jove.

In the 3rd century AD, the Christians redacted the Septuagint removing the name Iaô, both in Greek, and in Latin translations which transliterated Ιαω as Iaw, replacing it with 'Lord.' This resolved the debate with the Gnostics about whether Iaw was the devil or not. Before that, the various versions of the early Christian-era Septuagint books that included the name, either used Ιαω, or the name written in

Hebrew or Phoenician (Paleo-Hebrew) scripts. According to Origen of Alexandria in the late 2nd century AD, the Phoenician (most ancient script) was the most accurate. According to Theodoret of Cyprus in the 5th century, the Samaritans, who never switched to the Assyrian block letter 'Hebrew,' pronounced the name as Iabe (Ιαβε) or Iabae (Ιαβαι). Hebrews substitute the word 'hasheim,' meaning 'the name,' in all non-scriptural contexts since the Hasmoneans banned the pronunciation of the names of God. Christians have traditionally translated several ways including Jehovah, Jehova, and Jova. As the original Greek translation of Joshua does not appear to have included the name, the term Lord is used in this translation.

2 Codex Vaticanus: Bezec (ΒΕΖΕΚ)

• Aleppo Codex: bzq (בזק)

• Leningrad Codex: bezeq (בְזֶק)

• Targum Jerusalem: bezeq (בֶזֶק)

The location of Bezek is debated. Currently, the majority of scholars believe it was at the village of Ibziq in the northern Palestinian West Bank, while others had suggested it was at the nearby village of Salhab.

3 Codex Vaticanus: Adônibezec (ᴀᴅѡɴɪʙᴇᴢᴇκ)

- Aleppo Codex: ådny bzq (אדני בזק). Translation: Lord of Bezek

- Leningrad Codex: adoni bezeq (אֲדֹנִי בֶזֶק). Translation: Lord of Bezek

- Targum Jerusalem: adoni bezeq (אֲדֹנִי בֶזֶק). Translation: Lord of Bezek

While the Septuagint treats Adonibezec as a proper name, it is clear from the Masoretic Text that is was simply his title. The fact that this 'Lord' who had defeated 70 kings was not considered a king himself, supports the dating for the invasion of southern Canaan circa 1500 BC, after Pharaoh Thutmose's armies had passed through the territory, and the local chieftains had sworn allegiance to him. As the region was in chaos between the collapse of the Hyksos Dynasty circa 1540 BC, and the Pharaoh Thutmose's army pacifying the region in 1505 BC, it is entirely possible that a would-be successor to the Hyksos may have captured and mutilated 70 other would-be kings, before submitting to the Egyptians and consolidating his position within the new empire as a local lord.

4 Codex Vaticanus: Cariatharboxepher (κᴀᴘɪᴀөᴀᴘʙᴏᴢᴇɸᴇᴘ)

- Codex Alexandrinus: Cariatharbocsepher (κᴀᴘɪᴀөᴀᴘʙᴏκсᴇɸᴇᴘ)

- Aleppo Codex: qryt årbô (קרית ארבע). Translation: Village of Labor

- Leningrad Codex: kiryat arba (קִרְיַת אַרְבַּע). Translation: Village of Labor

- Targum Jerusalem: kiryat arba (קִרְיַת אַרְבַּע). Translation: Village of four

The Greek καριαθαρβοξεφερ and καριαθαρβοκσεφερ are not transliterations of kiryat arba (קִרְיַת אַרְבַּע), but a transliteration of kiryat arba sefer (קִרְיַת אַרְבַּע סָפֶר), meaning 'village of working books,' or 'village of the library.' As the word was removed from the text after 200 BC, the Hasmoneans are the most likely redactors.

5 Codex Vaticanus: Cariathsôphar polis grammatôn (ΚΑΡΙΑΘΟCΩΦΑΡΠΟΛΙCΓΡΑΜΜΑΤΩΝ). Translation: Cariathsôphar, city of letters

- Codex Alexandrinus: Polis grammatôn (ΠΟΛΙC ΓΡΑΜΜΑΤΩΝ). Translation: City of Letters

- Aleppo Codex: qryt spr (קרית ספר). Translation: Village Book (or scroll)

- Leningrad Codex: kiryat-sefer (קִרְיַת־סֵפֶר). Translation: Village Book (or scroll)

- Targum Jerusalem: kiryat archei (קִרְיַת אַרְכֵי). Translation: Village of Arke

The Greek καριαθσωφαρ is a transliteration of the Hebrew term found in the Masoretic Text. The Greeks added a translation 'city of the letters,' meaning they considered the name of the town to imply a communications hub. These two cities being burnt imply that the Judeans and Simeonites were targeting centers for higher learning within Canaan. These towns would have likely served as the main communications centers, as, prior to telegraphs being invented in the 1800s AD, the primary form of long-distance communication was letters. Cities where scribes studied writing and pigeon handling were found throughout the Middle East and the Mediterranean, such as Sumerian (and later Babylonian) Zimbar (later Sippar), a name also translating a 'Letters,' in Babylonian, although originally meaning 'birds' in Sumerian.

6 Codex Vaticanus: Iothor tou Cinaeou tou gambrou Môyseôs (ΙΟΘΟΡΤΟΥΚΙΝΑΙΟΥΤΟΥΓΑΜΒΡΟΥ ΜΩΥCΕΩC). Translation: Jethro the Kenite the son-in-law of Moses

• Codex Alexandrinus: Iôbab tou Cinaeou pentherou Môysê (ΙΩΒΑΒ ΤΟΥ ΚΙΝΑΙΟΥ ΠΕΝΘΕΡΟΥ ΜΩΥCΗ). Translation: Jobab the Kenite father-in-law of Moses

• Aleppo Codex: qyny htn mšh (קיני חתן משה). Translation: smith (or metalworker) son-in-law (or brother-in-law) of Moses

• Leningrad Codex: keini choten Mosheh (קֵינִי חֹתֵן מֹשֶׁה).
Translation: smith (or metalworker) son-in-law (or brother-in-law) of Moses

• Targum Jerusalem: Shalma'ah chamuhi deMosheh
(שֶׁלְמָאָה חָמוּהִי דְמֹשֶׁה). Translation: Shalmaite (Arabic tribe) of
the house of (or his daughter's father-in-law) of Moses

Three variations of this text are known, two in the
Septuagint codices, and one in the Masoretic Text. The two
Septuagint versions name the man in question as either
Jethro (Ιοθορ) or Jobab (Ιωβαβ), while the Masoretic Text
omits the name. The one version of the Septuagint and the
Masoretic Text agree that he was Moses' son-in-law or
brother-in-law (Γαμβρου / חֹתֵן), while the other Septuagint
version claims father-in-law (Πενθερου). Of all these sources,
the Codex Vaticanus is the oldest, dating to the 4th century
AD, which calls him Jethro the blacksmith son-in-law of
Moses.

The Codex Alexandrinus dates to the 5th century AD and is
believed to be based on the revision made by Lucian the
Martyr circa 300 AD, who redacted the Septuagint to make it
more like the Hebrew texts that were then in circulation.
Strangely, the Codex Alexandrinus claims Jobab was Moses'
father-in-law, while the Masoretic Text claims the unnamed
blacksmith was Moses' son-in-law. As the Masoretic Text omit
the name, there were likely different versions of Judges in
circulation at the time the Masorites began copying the text,
and they omitted the name in order to not pass on the wrong
name. Regardless of what the Masoretic Text state, almost all

English translations of them, refer to this blacksmith as Moses' father-in-law.

As two of the sources, Codex Vaticanus and the Masoretic Text agree he was Moses' son-in-law, the term son-in-law is used in this translation. Additionally, Moses' father-in-law Jethro was not a blacksmith, but a shepherd, and therefore it seems clear that Moses married his daughter to a blacksmith, although that story has not survived to the present. The man is named both Jethro and Jobab in this chapter of the surviving Septuagint codices, however, all three source texts call him 'Jobab the son-in-law of Moses' in Judges chapter 4.

7 Codex Vaticanus: poleôs tôn phoenicôn (ΠΟΛΕѠϹ ΤѠΝ ΦΟΙΝΙΚѠΝ). Translation: city the Phoenicians (or palm trees, dates, Phoenix)

- Aleppo Codex: môyr htmrym (מְעִיר הַתְּמָרִים). Translation: dates (or date palm trees in Hebrew), or blinking (in Aramaic)
- Leningrad Codex: me'ir hattemarim (מְעִיר הַתְּמָרִים). Translation: dates (or date palm trees)
- Targum Jerusalem: karta Yericho (קַרְתָּא יְרִיחוֹ). Translation: city of Jericho

As this flows from the Judahites capturing the 'city of letters,' suggesting that 'city of palm trees' was an alternate translation of the same location. The term used in the Masoretic Text is Hebrew, however, the word was adopted into Hebrew from the Aramaic word tmrå (תֹמְרָא) in the Iron Age, meaning it cannot have been the name used in the text before the Phoenician translation was made in the Kingdom of Samaria or Israel in the early Iron Age. The translator of the Targum Jerusalem seems to have recognized the anachronism, and substituted 'Jericho.' If 'palm' was the alternate translation of 'letters,' it suggests the Phoenician translation of Judges was made from an Egyptian language text, as 'book,' 'scroll,' 'papyrus,' and 'palm plants' was the same word in Egyptian: båt (𓃀𓄿𓏏), while the words were not synonyms in Semitic languages.

8 Codex Vaticanus: Anathema (ΑΝΑΘΕΜΑ)

- Codex Alexandrinus: Hexolethreusis (ΕΞΟΛΕΘΡΕΥCΙC)

- Aleppo Codex: ḥrmh (חרמה). Translation: the highlands (or the heights)

- Leningrad Codex: charemah (חָרְמָה). Translation: the highlands (or the heights)

- Targum Jerusalem: charemah (חָרְמָה). Translation: destruction

As all three source texts use a different name, the name Anathema is used from the Codex Vaticanus, the oldest of the surviving translations.

9 Codex Vaticanus: Rêchab (ΡΗΧΑΒ)

• Aleppo Codex: rkb brzl (רכב ברזל). Translation: chariots of iron

• Leningrad Codex: rekeb barzel (רֶכֶב בַּרְזֶל). Translation: chariots of iron

• Targum Jerusalem: detichin devarzela (דְּתִיכִין דְּבַרְזְלָא). Translation: in the judgment of iron

The Greek translation, Masoretic text, and Targum Jerusalem each interpret this sentence quite differently. The Greek translation interpreted Rechab as the name of a town or people, and is likely the same town or people mentioned in Psalms chapter 86 as Raab (Ρααβ), which was listed alongside other lands and cities that had defeated the Israelites, including Babylon, Tyre, Kush, and the Philistines. The term shows up in the parallel verse in the Masoretic Text as rhb (רהב), generally transliterated as Rahob, which was also the name of a sea monster in ancient Israelite myths. The prophet Isaiah, who lived around the time that the Phoenician translation of Judges was probably made, also used the term to refer to Egypt, suggesting the original text read that 'Egypt' had stopped Judah from destroying the people living in the valley. The translators of the Septuagint also translated rhb (רהב) as Cetus (Κητη) in Job chapter 9, indicating that they viewed Rechab as the ancient Israelite asterism of Cetus. Another term also translated as Cetus was Tanninim (תַּנִּינָם) in Genesis which was also translated as dragons (δρακοντα) in Psalms, while the term Livyatan

(לִוְיָתָן), generally transliterated as Leviathan was also translated as a dragon (δρακων).

The term Leviathan was used in the book of Isaiah, in a reference to the Ugaritic Texts which substituted the name Leviathan for Lotan. As such, this verse could the read either as the people of a town named Rêchab (Ρηχαβ) repulsing the Israelite attack, or the Egyptians forbidding the attack, or the god-monster itself defeating them, and presumably their god. Clearly, the Hasmonean redactors did not like this implication, and so changed this to read rkb brzl (רכב ברזל), meaning either chariots of iron, or the Egyptian's iron, depending on the interpretation of rekeb (רֶכֶב).

The translator of the Targum Jerusalem seemed to have recognized the double meaning of rekeb, and therefore substituted 'the judgment of iron' (דְתִיכִין דְבַרְזְלָא), however, iron is generally not viewed as being in wide use before the beginning of the iron age, and so these 'iron chariots,' are often viewed as an anachronism. If the 'iron chariots' were part of an older version of the story which had been lost in the Aramaic translation that the Greeks worked from, the 'iron' was probably the metal the ancient Egyptians called djôm (🜍 ⋯), which they recorded building chariots from during the New Kingdom era. Egyptologists generally believe this metal was electrum, as it is reported as coming from the 'gold' mines of southeast Egypt, where the 'gold' veins are rich in silver. The Egyptians had separate terms for both gold and silver, and referred to djôm as if it was some other kind of metal. As the gold veins in the region also contain small amounts of iron and nickle, it is possible that djôm was the residue left over from smelting the gold and sliver out of the raw metal, meaning that 'iron' would be an appropriate translation.

The New Kingdom king Tutankhamen was buried with an iron-nickel dagger, indicating that the residue from the gold and silver processing was being used to make weaponry during the New Kingdom era, however, it has not been proven that this was the metal known as djôm which was used to make chariots. Additionally, the Egyptians were smithing iron mined at Site 200 in the Timna Valley, in southern Israel's Arabah region during the New Kingdom era, presumably for weaponry. Nevertheless, it is more likely that the original reference was simply to Egypt itself, and the term 'iron' was an addition made in the early classical era, as the Greeks certainly knew what iron was, and would have translated it if it was in the texts they worked from, and it is improbable that the Aramaic translator would have removed the word.

10 Codex Vaticanus: Baethêl (ΒΑΙΘΗΛ)

- Aleppo Codex: byt ål (בית אל). Translation: house (or temple) of El (or god), Baitylos (or meteorite)

- Leningrad Codex: beit-El (בֵּית־אֵל). Translation: house (or temple) of El (or god), Baitylos (or meteorite)

- Targum Jerusalem: veit El (בֵית אֵל). Translation: house (or temple) of El

The term Bethel meant several things in ancient Canaan. The term translates as 'house of god,' which can be translated as either 'Temple of God/El' or 'sky/heaven.' Bethel was worshiped as a god by the ancient Canaanites, the brother of El and Dagon according to Sanchuniathon, who referred to him as Baitylos, which is the name used in this translation when the god. The term can also be translated as 'meteorite' as meteorites were believed to be parts of the god Baitylos that had fallen to the Earth, and shrines were built around them.

11 Codex Vaticanus: Louza (ΛΟΥΖΑ)

- Aleppo Codex: Lwz (לוז)

- Leningrad Codex: Luz (לוֹז)

- Targum Jerusalem: Luz (לוז)

The Samaritan city at the foot of Mount Gerizim is still known as Luza.

12 Codex Vaticanus: Chettiin (ΧΕΤΤΙΙΝ)

- Codex Alexandrinus: Chettiim (ΧΕΤΤΙΙΜ)

- Aleppo Codex: Ḥtym (חתים). General Translation: Cypriots

- Leningrad Codex: Chittim (חִתִּים). Translation: Cypriots

- Targum Jerusalem: Chitta'ei (חִתָּאֵי). Translation: Cypriots

This term has created a great deal of confusion since the misidentification of the ruins of the Neshites as being 'Hittite' in the 1800s. The modern archaeological name 'Hittite,' is not derived from an ancient name for the culture applied by themselves, or anyone else, but rather adopted from the biblical reference to a then-unknown civilization somewhere in the region. There was an ancient culture in the region called the Hattians, however, they were conquered by the Nesites before 1700 BC, and subsequently disappeared from the historic records. The name was applied to culture today referred to as 'Hittites,' before the 'Hittite' language had been translated, and is incorrect. Since 1906, excavations at Boğazköy, the ancient 'Hittite' capital Hattusa have uncovered more than 10,000 'Hittite' texts, including the royal achieve. The actual name of the 'Hittite' language and people was Nešili (𒉈𒅆𒇷), which is now rendered in some academic literate as Nesite or Neshite. As early as the mid-1800s some scholars disputed the identification of the Nesites as the Biblical Hittites, including the Orientalist Max Müller, who was one of many claiming the Biblical Hittites were ancient Greeks or some other Mediterranean people.

Later in the Septuagint's translation of the Maccabees, the similar term Chettiim (Χεττιιμ) as a reference to all Greek-speaking lands, and therefore the Biblical Hittites were likely the Minoans or the Achaean Greeks. In the 1st century AD, the Jewish historian Josephus reported that Cethima was the name of Cyrus in Aramaic, and the Chettim were the descendants of Noah's grandson Chethimus, who had settled on Cyprus. Josephus reported that the name was preserved in the Greek name of the town Cition (Κίτιον). Most historians view it as more likely that the Aramaic name was derived from the city-state of Cition, which was known as Kåtjåy (𓈎𓏏𓃀𓇌𓄿) in Egyptian records from the New Kingdom Era in the late Bronze Age, and Kt (𐤊𐤕) or Kty (𐤊𐤕𐤉) in Phoenician records from the early Iron Age. While this may be the origin of the term, by the era of the Neo-Assyrian era, the term must have also referred to other Greek islands, as both the prophets Isaiah and Ezekiel used the term 'Islands of Kittim.' As the term referred to the entire island of Cyprus in Aramaic, the translations of 'Cyprus' and 'Cypriots' are used here.

13 Codex Vaticanus: Louza (ΛΟΥΖΑ)

- Aleppo Codex: Lwz (לוז)

- Leningrad Codex: Luz (לוּז)

- Targum Jerusalem: Luz (לוז)

The Greek spelling of Louza (Λουζα) is a transliteration of the Aramaic spelling of the name, Lwzå (לוזא), indicating the Greek translation was made from an Aramaic source text. It is not clear which city of Luz/Louza the man built. There are a number of ancient cities across the Mediterranean bearing the name, including the Minoan city of Liso/Lissus (Λισο/Λισσος) on Crete, the ancient Greek city of Laüs (Λαος) in southern Italy, and the ancient Portuguese town of Lousã, as well as ancient records of towns with similar names in Carthaginian Tunisia and Algeria. The town of Liso in Crete is believed to date back to late-Minoan times, before 1100 BC, making it the most likely city being referred to.

The Canaanites (Phoenicians and Carthaginians) were present in southern Italy, northwest Africa, and Iberia long before the Greeks, however, it is not clear that any of the other settlements date back to before 1000 BC. The Greeks had occupied Laüs before 500 BC, however, it is not clear who founded the city or when. Ruins of the Portuguese town of Lousã have been found dating back to the Roman era, and the locations of the towns in Tunisia and Algeria are no longer known.

14 Codex Vaticanus: Baethsan (ΒΑΙΘϹΑΝ)

• Aleppo Codex: byt šån (בּית שאן). Translation: House (or temple) of She'an

• Leningrad Codex: beit-She'an (בֵּית־שְׁאָן). Translation: House (or temple) of She'an

• Targum Jerusalem: beit She'an (בֵּית שְׁאָן). Translation: House (or temple) of wishes

The city of Beth She'an was officially annexed by the Egyptians around 1457 BC, when the army of Thutmose III occupied Canaan en route to Syria. The city was an Egyptian city in Canaan until the collapse of the Egyptian New Kingdom, circa 1150 BC, when the city was burnt down. It was rebuilt a few decades later as a Canaanite city and the ruins of the new city show no evidence of being culturally connected to Egypt. The Assyrians burnt down the city again when they occupied Samaria circa 732 BC, and it remained largely unoccupied until sometime in the Persian era, when Scythians settled at the site, resulting in the Greek name Scythopolis.

While the Greeks added the reference to the contemporary name of Scythopolis, the Masoretic Text does not include that reference, and the city in question is the city of Beth She'an that was burned down in 1150 BC. The book of Judge's claims that Beth She'an was not occupied by the Israelites is true, the Egyptians recorded that the city was under their control and there are no records of it being attacked. These Egyptian records are found on the monuments in Karnak and are supported by the archaeological evidence of an Egyptian city at the site between 1450 and 1150 BC. Based on the Egyptian records, the main god worshiped at the Beth She'an was a god called Mekal, which appears to be a precursor to the Jewish messenger Michael.

15 Codex Vaticanus: Thanak (ΘΑΝΑΚ).

- Codex Alexandrinus: Ecthanaad (ΕΚΘΑΝΑΑΔ)

- Aleppo Codex: Tônk (תַעֲנַךְ)

- Leningrad Codex: Ta'nach (תַּעֲנַךְ)

- Targum Jerusalem: Ta'anach (תַּעֲנָךְ)

As the Codex Vaticanus and Masoretic Text agree, most translations of the Septuagint prefer the name Thanak (or

Taanach) over Ecthanaad. The modern village is called Ti'inik, and is located in the northern-most region of the Palestinian West Bank. Ti'inik was occupied by the Egyptians between 1457 and 1150 BC.

16 Codex Vaticanus: Dôr (ܕܘܪ)

- Aleppo Codex: Dwr (דור)

- Leningrad Codex: Dor (דּוֹר)

- Targum Jerusalem: Dor (דוֹר)

The city of Dor was occupied by the Egyptians during the New Kingdom era, between 1457 and 1150 BC. The city of Djr (𓂧𓏭𓂋𓈉) was mentioned in several Egyptian texts from the New Kingdom era, and featured in the Voyage of Wenamen set circa 1050 BC, after the city had broken away from Egyptian control. The city was located as the mound today called Tel Dor on the Mediterranean coast of Israel between Haifa and Hadera.

17 Codex Vaticanus: Balak (ΒΑΛΑΚ)

- Codex Alexandrinus: Balaam (ΒΑΛΑΑΜ)

- Aleppo Codex: Yblôm (יבלעם)

- Leningrad Codex: Yivle'am (יִבְלְעָם)

- Targum Jerusalem: Yivle'am (יְבְלְעָם)

The Septuagint's list of cities also includes Ieblaam (Ιεβλααμ) at the end, which also appears to be a transliteration of Yivle'am (יִבְלְעָם) from the Masoretic Text As Belameh (Βαλααμ / בְּלְעָם) also appears at the end of the list, Balak is used in this translation. The name Balak (Βαλακ) appears to be a translation of the Hebrew name Balak (בָּלָק), which was the name of the Moabite king in Numbers, which implies the land of Balak was Moab. Moab was occupied by the Egyptians during the New Kingdom, however, does not appear in their records until the Canaanite campaigns of Ramesses II circa 1275 BC. By the time of Ramesses II, Moab was a petty kingdom allied to Egypt, however, it is likely that it was officially annexed in 1457 BC when Thutmose III's armies annexed the rest of Canaan.

18 Codex Vaticanus: Magedô (ΜΑΓΕΔΩ)

• Codex Alexandrinus: Magedôn (ΜΑΓΕΔΩΝ)

• Aleppo Codex: Mgdw (מגדו)

• Leningrad Codex: Megiddov (מְגִדּוֹ)

• Targum Jerusalem: Megido (מְגִדוֹ)

The town of Megiddo was listed as a town occupied by the armies of Thutmose III's army in 1457 BC. Some records from Megiddo have survived among the Amarna Letters. Amarna Letter EA245 mentioned the governor Biridiya, from circa 1350 BC.

19 Codex Vaticanus: Ieblaam (ιεв∧∧∧м)

The Masoretic Text does not contain another name after Meggido in this list, however, the Greek Ieblaam (Ιεβλααμ), which is found in both the Vaticanus and Alexandrinus versions of Judges, appears to be a translation of yiVle'am (יִבְלְעָם), meaning 'of Vle'am,' which is listed earlier in the Masoretic Text. The city of Balaam is generally accepted as the city of Belameh, listed as one of the towns occupied by Pharaoh Thutmose III's army circa 1450 BC. The town was occupied throughout Israelite and Judahite history, and was known as Belemoth during the Greco-Roman era.

20 Codex Vaticanus: Dômana (∆ωм∧N∧)

- Codex Alexandrinus: Enaala (εN∧∧∧∧)

- Aleppo Codex: Nhll (נהלל)

- Leningrad Codex: Nahalol (נַהֲלֹל)

- Targum Jerusalem: Nahalol (נַהֲלֹל)

The Codex Alexandrinus' Enaala appears to be a transliteration of the Hebrew Nahalal, however, was most likely part of Lucian's redaction circa 300 AD, meaning the original Septuagint probably used the name Domana. There is an Israeli community called Nahalal in northern Israel today, however, there is no archaeological evidence connecting it to the ancient settlement.

21 Codex Vaticanus: Dôr (ܐܘܿܪ)

The Masoretic Text does not mention Dor a second time here, however, it was previously listed among the cities that Manasseh did not drive the inhabitants out of.

22 Codex Vaticanus: Sidôna (ܣܝܕܘܿܢܐ)

- Aleppo Codex: Sydwn (צִידּוֹן)

- Leningrad Codex: Tzidovn (צִידֹון)

- Targum Jerusalem: Tzidovn (צִידֹון)

Sidon (𐤑𐤃𐤍) was one of the most ancient Canaanite cities, and arguably the mother-city of all of Canaanite culture. Tyre also claimed to be Phoenicia's mother-city, however, it was originally a colony of Sidon. Egyptian records from the 1300s BC listed the city as Djedunå (𓂧𓆑𓈖𓇋) while it was part of the Egyptian New Kingdom. It was likely occupied by Thutmose III with the rest of Canaan in 1457 BC.

23 Greek: Aalaph (ΑΑΛΑΦ)

- Aleppo Codex: Åhlb (אחלב)

- Leningrad Codex: Achlav (אַחְלָב)

- Targum Jerusalem: Achlav (אַחְלָב)

24 Codex Vaticanus: Aschazi (ΑϹΧΑΖΙ)

- Codex Alexandrinus: Achazib (ΑΧΑΖΙΒ)

- Aleppo Codex: Åkzyb (אכזיב)

- Leningrad Codex: Achziv (אַכְזִיב)

- Targum Jerusalem: Achziv (אַכְזִיב)

Achzib was a major Canaanite city during the Egyptian New Kingdom Era. It was originally built between two rivers, however, by the Middle Bronze Age, the city extended from one river to the other, and the Canaanites dug a moat between the two rivers, effectively making the city into an island. The city was later transferred to King Hiram of Tyre by King Solomon and appears to have been independent of Israelite (Samaritan and Judahites) control until the Assyrians conquered it in 701 BC under King Sennacherib. The city of Achzib was located along the Mediterranean coast of modern Israel, north of Acre.

25 Codex Vaticanus: Nai (ΝΑΙ)

- Codex Alexandrinus: Aphec (ΑΦΕΚ)

- Aleppo Codex: Åpyq (אפיק)

- Leningrad Codex: Afik (אֲפִיק)

- Targum Jerusalem: Afik (אֲפִיק)

The Codex Alexandrinus' Aphec appears to be a transliteration of the Hebrew åpyq, however, was most likely part of Lucian's redaction circa 300 AD, meaning the original Septuagint probably used the name Nai.

26 Codex Vaticanus: Ereô (єρєယ)

- Codex Alexandrinus: Roôb (ροယв)

- Aleppo Codex: Rḥb (רחב)

- Leningrad Codex: Rechov (רְחֹב)

- Targum Jerusalem: Rechov (רְחוֹב)

This location is not known today. There are the remains of another place called Rehob near Beth She'an, however, the ruins in question are not believed to be associated with this Rehob. There is also not an ancient site known as Ereo. The general assumption is that the location of this Rehob (or Ereo) was in Lebanon somewhere. As the name Roôb found in the Codex Alexandrinus is likely part of Lucian's redaction, and Ereo was likely the original name in the Septuagint, Ereo is used in this translation.

27 Greek: Baethsamys (вліөсамүс)

- Aleppo Codex: Byt Šmš (בית שמש). Translation: house (or temple) of Shemesh (or sun)

- Leningrad Codex: veit-Shemesh (בֵית-שֶׁמֶשׁ). Translation: house (or temple) of Shemesh (or sun)

• Targum Jerusalem: veit Shemesh (בֵית שֶׁמֶשׁ). Translation: house (or temple) of Shemesh (or sun)

The modern city of Beit Shemesh (بيت شيمش / בֵית שֶׁמֶשׁ) is located near the ancient site of the town, today called Tel Beit Shemesh. Shemesh was the Canaanite sun god, influenced by the Mesopotamian solar-god Shamesh. King Josiah of Judah banned the worship of Shemesh in circa 625 BC, along with the other Canaanite and early Israelite gods.

28 Codex Vaticanus: Baethanath (ΒΑΙΘΑΝΑΘ)

• Codex Alexandrinus: Baetheneth (ΒΑΙΘΕΝΕΘ)

• Aleppo Codex: Byt ônt (בית ענת). Translation: house (or temple) of Anat

• Leningrad Codex: veit-Anat (בֵית־עֲנָת). Translation: house (or temple) of Anat

• Targum Jerusalem: veit Anat (בֵית עֲנָת). Translation: house (or temple) of Anat

The location of Beth Anat is unknown today. Sites have been suggested in Lebanon, Galilee, and at the foot of Mount Hermon. Anat (𐤏𐤍𐤕) was a war goddess, and one of the major deities of Canaan. Anat was one of the key motivators of her brother Ba'al Hadad's rebellion against Yam (Sea) in the Canaanite Ba'al Cycle literature, dated to between 1450 and 1200 BC. She was also central to Ba'al's resurrection during his conflict with Mot (Death). Her worship had already been imported to Egypt during the Second Intermediate Period, currently dated to between 1650 and 1580 BC, and was part of Pharaoh Anat-Har's name, showing how important she was at the time.

She was integrated into the Egyptian pantheon as the daughter of Ptah, the creator-god. It is unclear which dynasty Anat-Har was a Pharaoh of, however, his name suggests he was a Canaanite or Hyksos Pharaoh. There are remains of temples dedicated to her dating from the Hyksos Dynasty in the ruins of Avaris (later Pi-Ramesses, and then Ramesses) and Memphis (now Cairo) in Egypt, and Beth She'an (later called Scythopolis) in Israel. The Temple of Anat in Avaris was taken over by later dynasties and expanded within the renamed city of Pi-Ramesses, and she continued to be a major Egyptian goddess throughout the New Kingdom. Anat later became synonymous with her Canaanite title Qetesh in Canaan, although Qetesh was adopted as a separate Goddess by the Egyptians. Qetesh was widely worshiped by the Israelites before King Josiah banned her worship in Judah circa 625 BC. The name Anat continued to be used by the Israelites in addition to her title Qetesh (Holiness), and was treated as the wife of Yahw (Yehvah) until at least the 5th century BC, as evidenced by the Elephantine papyri, which listed her as Anat-Yahw.

29 Codex Vaticanus: ori tô ostracôdi (ΟΡΕΙΤѠ ΟϹΤΡΑΚѠΔΕΙ). Translation: Mountains of earth (or pottery)

• Codex Alexandrinus: ori tou Myrsinônos (ΟΡΕΙ ΤΟΥ ΜΥΡΣΙΝѠΝΟC). Translation: Mountains of Myrsinônos (or myrtle)

• Aleppo Codex: bhr ḥrs (בהר חרס). Translation: mountain of destruction (or clay)

• Leningrad Codex: behar-cheres (בְּהַר־חֶרֶס). Translation: mountain of destruction (or clay)

• Targum Jerusalem: tur cheres (טוּר חֶרֶס). Translation: Mount Heres

As the name Codex Vaticanus is similar to the 'Mount Heres' of the Masoretic Text, that name is imported. However, it is not entirely clear what the name Heres means, as it is sometimes a reference to the underworld in Canaanite literature, but sometimes a reference to the sun or a sun-god in early Israelite literature. This may be an alternate or earlier translation of the northern Mount Hor from the Book of Joshua.

30 Codex Vaticanus: Myrsinôni (ΜΥΡΣΙΝѠΝΙ)

• Codex Alexandrinus: does not mention the Μυρσινωνι Mountains a second time, however, does mention the name earlier in the verse.

• Aleppo Codex: Åylwn (אילון)

• Leningrad Codex: Ayyalovn (אַיָּלוֹן)

• Targum Jerusalem: Ayalon (אַיְלוֹן)

Ajalon was listed by Governor Adbi-Heba of Jerusalem as a town destroyed by invaders in the El-Amarna Letters circa 1330 BC. Prior to this, the town was considered Egyptian territory, however, this attack on Ayalon appears to be part of an ongoing process of territorial losses by the New Kingdom. Pharaoh Sheshonk I recaptured the region in 925 BC after the collapse of the United Kingdom of Israel.

31 Codex Vaticanus: Thalabin (ΘΑΛΑΒΙΝ).

• Codex Alexandrinus: does not mention the name Thalabin, Shaalbim, or any other variation in this verse.

• Aleppo Codex: Šôlbym (שַׁעֲלְבִים)

• Leningrad Codex: Sha'alvim (שַׁעַלְבָים)

• Targum Jerusalem: Sha'alvim (שַׁעֲלְבִים)

The ruins near the modern Israeli town of Šôlbym are believed to be the ruins of Shaalbim. As the Greek Thalabin appears to be a transliteration of Shaalbim, and the modern town is called Sha'alvim, that name is used in this translation.

32 Codex Vaticanus: Acrabin (ΑΚΡΑΒΙΝ)

• Aleppo Codex: ôqrbym (עֲקְרַבִים). Translation: scorpions

• Leningrad Codex: akrabbim (עַקְרַבִּים). Translation: scorpions

• Targum Jerusalem: akra bim (עֲקַר בִּים). Translation: barren (or sterile) among

The location of the Ascent of Akrabbim has been debated for over 2000 years. The 1ˢᵗ century AD Jewish historian Flavius Josephus described the Ascent of Akrabbim as lying between Judea and Galilee in Samaria in *The Wars of the Jews* circa 75 AD:

> Now as to the country of Samaria, it lies between Judea and Galilee; it begins at a village that is in the great plain called Ginea, and ends at the Acrabbene toparchy, and is entirely of the same nature with Judea; for both countries are made up of hills and valleys, and are moist enough for agriculture, and are very fruitful.

33 Codex Vaticanus: Petras (ΠΕΤΡΑϹ). Translation: Petra (or stone)

• Aleppo Codex: Slô (סְלַע). Translation: stone

• Leningrad Codex: Sela (סָּרְלַע). Translation: stone

• Targum Jerusalem: keifa (כֵּיפָא). Translation: pressure

It is not clear from the Masoretic Text if the original author intended the city of Petra or not, however, the Greek translators did translate the term as the name of the city. The 1ˢᵗ century AD Jewish historian Flavius Josephus located the Torah's Kadesh Barnea at Petra, which would mean that Petra was in the Hebrew texts before the era of Judges. A town called Sela was listed in the Amarna Letters from circa 1330 BC, which appears to be Petra. In the Amarna Letters, Sela was occupied by the Egyptians, however, does not appear to have been part of the Egyptian Empire before that time.

Judges: Chapter 2

The messenger of the lord[1] went up from the circle[2] to Bokim,[3] the Temple of El, and to the Temple of Israel,[4] and said to them, "The Lord says, 'I brought you up out of Egypt, and I brought you into the land which I swore to your fathers and I promised, "I will never break my covenant that I have made with you. You will make no covenant with those that live in this land, neither will you worship their gods. Instead, you will destroy their carved images, you will pull down their altars." But, you did not listen to my voice, and you did these things, and I said, "I will not drive them out from before you, but they will be distresses to you, and their gods will be an offense to you.""'"

When the messenger of the lord spoke these words to the Israelites, the people raised their voices and wept. They renamed that place Bokim. They sacrificed to the Lord there, and Joshua dismissed the people, and they went each man to his inheritance, to inherit the land. The people served the Lord all the days of Joshua, and all the days of the elders that lived many days with Joshua, as many as knew all the great works of the Lord, what things he had worked in Israel. Joshua the son of Nun, the servant of the Lord, died at a hundred and ten years old. They buried him in the border of his inheritance, in Timnath Heres, in the mountains of Ephraim, on the north side of Mount Gaash. All that generation was laid with their fathers, and another generation rose up after them, who did not know the Lord, nor the work which he did for Israel. The Israelites worked evil before the Lord and served the Ba'als.[5] They forgot the Lord God[6] of their fathers, who brought them out of the land of Egypt, and followed other gods, the gods of the nations around them, and they worshiped them. They provoked the Lord, and forgot him, and served Ba'al[7] and Astarte.[8] The Lord was very angry with Israel, and he gave them into the hands of plunderers, and they ruined them. He sold them into the hands of their enemies around them, and they could no longer resist their enemies, among whoever they went, and the hand of the Lord was evilly against them. As the Lord had promised, and as the Lord had sworn to them, he punished them greatly. Then the Lord raised up judges, and the Lord saved them out of the hands of those that plundered them, and yet they did not listen to the judges, and they went whoring after other gods and worshiped them. They turned quickly from how their fathers walked when they listen to the words of the Lord. The Lord raised judges among them, and the Lord was with the judges and saved them out of the hand of their enemies all the days of the judges because the Lord was moved by their moaning caused by those that besieged them and attacked them. When the judges died, they went back and again corrupted themselves worse than their fathers, going after other gods to serve them and to worship them. They did not abandon their devices or their stubborn ways. The Lord was very angry with Israel, and said, "Since this nation has forgotten my covenant which I commanded their fathers, and has not listened to my voice, I will never again drive out a man from the nations in front of them, which Joshua the son of Nun left in the land."

The Lord left them to see if Israel would keep the way of the Lord, and follow it like their fathers had or not. So the Lord left these nations and did not drive them out suddenly, and he did not deliver them into the hand of Joshua.

Judges: Chapter 2 Notes

1 Codex Vaticanus: angelos cyriou (ᴀᴦᴦᴇᴧᴏᴄᴋ¥ᴘιᴏ¥).
Translation: messenger lord

- Aleppo Codex: mlåk Yhwh (מלאך יהוה). Translation:
messenger Yhwh

- Leningrad Codex: mal'ach-Yehvah (מַלְאַךְ־יְהוָה).
Translation: messenger Yehwah

- Targum Jerusalem: kodam Yeyah (קֳדָם יי). Translation:
advance of Yahw

2 Codex Vaticanus: Galgal (ᴦᴧᴧᴦᴧᴧ)

- Aleppo Codex: glgl (גלגל). Translation: circle

- Leningrad Codex: gilgal (גִּלְגָּל). Translation: circle

- Targum Jerusalem: gilgela (גִּלְגְּלָא)

Gilgal (גִּלְגָּל) is the Hebrew word for circle. Archaeologists
have discovered several ceremonial stone circles in Canaan
that were used between 1200 and 1000 BC for gatherings that
are assumed to be religious in nature. As these stone circles
are found down in the valleys, unlike the altars at the tops of
hills where the Canaanites worshiped, and 'circles' (גלגל) are
mentioned throughout the old Hebrew texts, it is assumed
they are early Israelite religious centers from before the First
Temple was built. According to the Book of Joshua, the
Israelites built a stone circle in Samaria after invading Canaan
in approximately 1508 BC.

3 Codex Vaticanus: Clauthmôna (ΚΛΑΥΘΜΩΝΑ).
Translation: weepings

• Aleppo Codex: bkym (בכים). Translation: cryings

• Leningrad Codex: bochim (בֹּכִים). Translation: cryings

• Targum Jerusalem: Bochim (בּוֹכִים)

As the Greek translation appears to be a translation of the Hebrew name, the Hebrew name is used in this translation.

4 Codex Vaticanus: oecon Israêl (ΟΙΚΟΝΙϹΡΑΗΛ).
Translation: home (or house, or temple) of Israel

This reference is missing from the Masoretic version of Judges, however, as it was referring to the Samaritan temple on or near Mount Gerizim, it would have been removed. Assuming this is part of the original text of Judges, it supports the Samaritan claim that the original Israelite temple built in Canaan was on Mount Gerizim, before the building of King Solomon's Temple. Conversely, this may be viewed as evidence that the Greeks translated a Samaritan copy of Judges, however, it is unlikely that any Samaritan copies have been translated into Aramaic, as the Samaritans never abandoned the old Canaanite dialect of Samaria or the Phoenician script.

5 Greek: Baalim (ʙⲁⲁⲗⲓⲙ)

• Aleppo Codex: bôlym (בְעלים). Translation: the lords (or the masters, the husbands)

• Leningrad Codex: be'alim (בְּעָלִים). Translation: the lords (or the masters, the husbands)

• Targum Jerusalem: ba'alaya (בַּעֲלִיָא). Translation: lords

The term Ba'al was an ancient Semitic term that was used to denote lords or gods of Canaan.

6 Codex Vaticanus: ton c̄n ton t̄hn (ⲦⲞⲚⲔⲚⲦⲞⲚⲈⲚ). Translation: the Lord the God

• Codex Alexandrinus: ton cyrion theon (ⲦⲞⲚⲔⲨⲣⲓⲟⲚ ⲐⲈⲞⲚ). Translation: the Lord God

• Aleppo Codex: åt yhwh ålhy (את יהוה אלהי). Translation: the Yhwh god

• Leningrad Codex: et-Yehvah | elohei (אֶת־יְהוָה \ אֱלֹהֵי). Translation: the Yehwah. God

• Targum Jerusalem: daYeyah elaha (דַיְיָ אֱלָהָא). Translation: from Yahw god

The name Yahw (𐤉𐤄𐤅) was transliterated as Iaô (Ιαω) in some books of the Septuagint, which was later transliterated as Iaw by the Pre-Christian Romans. In later copies of the Septuagint, the name was replaced by the name written in Canaanite (𐤉𐤄𐤅𐤄) or Assyrian script (יהוה). There are no early surviving copies of the Septuagint's version of Judges which have the name Iaô (Ιαω) in it, like some of the other books of the Septuagint, and therefore it cannot be proven conclusively if the name was in the Septuagint's Judges or not, however, a number of other books in the Septuagint appear to retain older versions of the Hebrew scriptures that pre-date the redaction during the Hasmonean dynasty, which replaced many older names of gods with Yehvah or Yehvah tzeva'ovt, the national god of Hasmonean Judea. The Aramaic sections of Masoretic Daniel that were not translated into Hebrew maintain the term adonai ha'elohim (אֲדֹנָי הָאֱלֹהִים), meaning the 'Lord the gods' where the Septuagint has 'Lord the god' (Κύριον τὸν θεὸν), however, the Hebrew sections have Yehvah elohim (יְהוָה אֱלֹהִים) where the Septuagint has 'Lord the god,' suggesting the Greek more accurately reflects the Aramaic source texts than the Hebrew translation.

According to tractate Sanhedrin (103b) in the Talmud, King Manasseh was blamed for removing the name, however, as his grandson Josiah 'restored' the Torah circa 625 BC, one would expect that he would have restored the name as well, if it had have been in Exodus to begin with. Furthermore, the early Torah appears to have already been translated into Aramaic during the era of Manasseh's father king Hezekiah, suggesting that he removed the name during his religious reforms.

7 Codex Vaticanus: Ba'al (ΒΑΑΛ)

- Aleppo Codex: bôl (בעל). Translation: lord (or master, or husband)

• Leningrad Codex: ba'al (בַּעַל). Translation: lord (or master, or husband)

• Targum Jerusalem: va'ala (בַעֲלָא). Translation: lord (or master, or husband)

While Baʻal was a title applied to many Canaanite gods, when used as a name, it referred to Baʻal Hadad, the storm god, and hero of the Baʻal Cycle literature of ancient Canaan.

8 Codex Vaticanus: Astartaes (ⲁⲥⲧⲁⲣⲧⲁⲓⲥ)

• Aleppo Codex: Ôštrwt (עשתרות)

• Leningrad Codex: Ashtarovt (עַשְׁתָּרוֹת)

• Targum Jerusalem: Ashtarata (עֲשְׁתַּרְתָא)

Astarte was the Greek name the Canaanite of Ashtoreth and Mesopotamian Ishtar. Ashtoreth was the Canaanite goddess of love, sex, war, and the planet Venus. Local versions of her were worshiped throughout the Middle East and the Mediterranean Sea. In Akkadian, he was a god known as Asdartu, while in Babylonia she was known as Ishtar, in Ugaritic she was known as ʻAthtart, and in Etruscan, she was known as Uni-Astre. The Greek goddess Aphrodite appears to be derived from an early version of her, while the Roman goddess appears to be derived indirectly through the Etruscan Uni-Astre. The Aramean transgender deity Atargatis appears to be another early offshoot that maintained the early male aspect of the god from the Akkadian era while accepting that the god had become a goddess. During the

New Kingdom era of Egyptian history, circa 1549 tom 1077 AD, Astarte was incorporated into the Egyptian pantheon as one of the daughters of Ra, as she appeared in the book entitled the 'Contest between Horus and Set.' According to the Phoenician scholar Sanchuniathon, who supposedly lived circa 1200 BC, Astarte's sister was Asherah, who was also known as Anat. The word Asherah also appears in the Septuagint many times and appears to be widely worshiped by the early Israelites.

Judges: Chapter 3

These are the nations which the Lord left to test Israel with, all that had not known the wars of Canaan, for the sake of the generations of Israel, to teach them war. The men before them did not know them. The five lords of the foreigners,[1] and all the Canaanites, Sidonians, and Mitanni[2] who lived in Lebanon from Mount Hermon[3] to the entrance of Hama.[4] This was done to test Israel, to know whether they would obey the commands of the Lord, which he ordered their fathers through the hand of Moses. The Israelites lived among the Canaanites, Cypriots, Amorites, Perizzites, Mitannians, and Jebusites. They took their daughters as wives for themselves, and they gave their daughters to their sons and served their gods.

The Israelites did evil in the sight of the Lord, and forgot the Lord God, and served Ba'als and Asherahs.[5] The Lord was very angry with Israel and sold them into the hand of the Kassite Barattarna,[6] king of the Syrian rivers,[7] and the Israelites served the Kassite Barattarna eight years. The Israelites cried to the Lord, and the Lord raised a savior for Israel, and he saved them, Othniel the son of Kenez, the younger brother of Caleb. The spirit of the Lord came on him, and he judged Israel, and he went out to war against the Kassite Barattarna, and the Lord delivered into his hand the Kassite Barattarna king of the Syrian rivers, and his hand prevailed against the

Kassite Barattarna. The land was peaceful for forty years, and Othniel the son of Kenez died.

The Israelites continued to do evil before the Lord, and the Lord strengthened Moab against Israel because they had done evil before the Lord. He gathered to himself all Ammonites and Amalekites, and went and attacked Israel, and occupied the city of palm-trees. The Israelites served Eglon the king of Moab for eighteen years. The Israelites cried to the Lord, and he raised for them a savior, Ehud the son of Gera, a Benjamite, a man who used both hands alike, and the Israelites sent gifts by his hand to Eglon king of Moab. Ehud made himself a double-edged dagger a span long, and he hid it under his cloak on his right thigh. He went and brought the presents to Eglon king of Moab, and Eglon was a very fat man.[8] When Ehud had finished offering his gifts, he dismissed those that brought the gifts. He returned from the quarries that were by the circle, and Ehud said, "I have a secret message for you, king!"

Eglon replied to him, "Be quiet, and he sent away from his presence all who waited on him."

Ehud went to him, and they sat in his upper summer chamber all alone, and Ehud said, "I have a message from God for you, my king," and Eglon rose up from his throne near him. As he arose, Ehud stretched out his left hand, and took the dagger from his right thigh, and plunged it into his stomach, and drove in also the haft behind the blade, and the fat closed in on the blade, as he did not pull out the dagger from his belly. Ehud went out to the porch, and collapsed out by the guards stationed there, and shut the doors of the chamber on him, and locked them. He went out, and Eglon's servants came and saw, and the doors of the upper chamber were locked, and they asked, "Does he not uncover his feet in the summer chamber? They waited until they were embarrassed, and no one opened the doors of the upper chamber. They took the key, and opened them, and found their lord had fallen dead on the ground.

Ehud escaped while they were in chaos, and no one paid attention to him, and he passed the quarries and escaped to Seirah.[9] It happened when Ehud came into the land of Israel, that he blew the horn on Mount Ephraim, and the Israelites came down with him from the mountain. He led them and said, "Come down after me, for the Lord God has delivered our enemies, Moab, into our hands!"

They went down after him and occupied the fords of the Jordan en route to Moab, and he did not allow a man to pass over. They slaughtered about ten thousand Moabites on that day, every lusty person and every mighty man, and not a man escaped. Moab was humbled on that day under the hand of Israel, and the land had peace for eighty years, and Ehud judged them until he died.

After him rose up Shamgar the son of Anat, and slaughtered six hundred Pelesets with a plowshare, like one drawn by oxen, and he too saved Israel.

Judges: Chapter 3 Notes

1 Greek: allophylôn (ⲁⲗⲗⲟ⳨ⲩⲗⲱⲛ). Translation: foreigners (or strangers, aliens)

• Aleppo Codex: plštym (פלשתים). Translation: Philistines (or Palestinians, Peleset)

• Leningrad Codex: Felishtim (פְּרִשְׁתִּים). Translation: Philistines (or Palestinians, Peleset)

• Targum Jerusalem: Pelishta'ei (פְּלִשְׁתָּאֵי). Translation: Philistines (or Palestinians, Peleset)

The Pelesets were an ancient people based in the region of the modern Gaza Strip of the Palestinian Territories. The earliest surviving mention of them is from the reliefs of the Temple of Ramses III at Medinet Habu in Egypt that dates back to some time between 1186 and 1155 BC, in which they were called Pelesets (𓊪𓃭𓏌𓈙𓏏𓀀). They were also known in Middle Babylonian as the ᵏᵘʳPalastu (𒆳𒉺𒆷𒊍𒌓). It is unclear where they came from, however, one theory is that they were the Pala, a Luwian people from the Black Sea coast of Anatolia. The region was an independent country called Palaa (𒉺𒆷𒀀) in the Neshite (Hittite) records from the 1600s BC, however, have become part of the Nesite Empire by the 1500s BC. Around the time the Pelesets invaded Canaan, the Pala were driven from their homeland by the neighboring Kaskians from northeast Anatolia, which supports the connection between the groups, however, it has yet to be proven conclusively.

The presence of the Pelesets in Southern Canaan during the time of Abraham and Isaac is anachronistic, and therefore this section of text, describing the origin of the Semitic tribes, found in both the Septuagint and the Masoretic Text, likely dates to the original Phoenician translation in the early Iron Age.

2 Greek: Euaion (ЄΥΑΙΟΝ)

* Aleppo Codex: Hwy (חוי)

* Leningrad Codex: Chivvi (חִוִּי)

* Targum Jerusalem: Chiva'ei (חִוָּאֵי). Translation: farmer

The term is believed to have been derived from the name of the Hurrians, however, is derived separately from the other term Chori (חֹרִי). As the Hivites are routinely reported to be rulers, the term appears to represent the Mitanni-Aryan nobility or Vedic priests. As the Mitanni Empire lost its Canaanite territory circa 1350 BC, the original text of Judges must date back to before that time.

3 Codex Vaticanus: orous tou Aermôn (ΟΡΟΥΣΤΟΥ ΑЄΡΜΩΝ). Translation: mountain of Hermon

* Codex Alexandrinus: orous tou Balaermôn (ΟΡΟΥΣΤΟΥ ΒΑΛΛАЄΡΜΩΝ). Translation: mountain of Balaermon

* Aleppo Codex: hr Bôl Hrmwn (הר בעל חרמון). Translation: mountain of Lord Hermon

- Leningrad Codex: har Ba'al Chermovn (הַר בַּעַל חֶרְמוֹן).
Translation: mountain of Lord Hermon

- Targum Jerusalem: tur meishar Chermovn (טוּר מֵישַׁר חֶרְמוֹן). Translation: mountain of the prince (or commander) of Hermon

The location of Ba'al-Hermon in the Masoretic Text and Codex Alexandrinus is unclear, however, the Codex Vaticanus indicates it was Mount Hermon, on the modern Israeli-Lebanese-Syrian border. Mount Hermon was the location where the Watchers descended to Earth in the Enochian Book of the Watchers. It is also the location of the Anaks in the Book of Joshua, which appears to be a reference to the descendants of the Watchers. The Egyptians listed a people known as the Anaq living in the region between 2300 and 1700 BC, which are accepted as being the same people the Israelites called the Anaks. The ruins of over 30 temples have been discovered on Mount Hermon, including a rock-cut temple of the summit called Qasr Antar, which may date back to the Anak civilization.

4 Codex Vaticanus: Labôemath (ΛΑΒWЄΜΑΘ)

- Codex Alexandrinus: Lobôêmath (ΛΟΒWΗΜΑΘ)

- Aleppo Codex: lbwå Hmt (לְבוֹא חמת). Translation: entrance to Hama

- Leningrad Codex: levov Chamat (לְבוֹא חֲמָת). Translation: entrance to Hama

• Targum Jerusalem: ma'alana daChamat (מַעֲלָנָא דַחֲמָת).
Translation: gateway of Hama

The Greeks transliterated the word meaning 'entrance' as part of the name, and therefore the Masoretic version of the name is used in this translation. Hama is a major city in western Syria north of Lebanon that had been inhabited since around 6000 BC. It was under the control of the Mitanni Empire between 1500 and 1350 BC.

5 Codex Vaticanus: toes alsesin (ΤΟΙϹΑΛϹΕϹΙΝ).
Translation: the sacred groves

• Aleppo Codex: ăšrwt (אשרות). Translation: Asherahs

• Leningrad Codex: Asherovt (אֲשֵׁרֹות). Translation: Asherahs

• Targum Jerusalem: Asharata (אֲשֵׁרָתָא). Translation: Asherahs

Asherah was the wife of the Canaanite god El, and Mesopotamian god An (Anu), and the mother of the Canaanite gods. The Asherahs in question were likely sacred oak trees dedicated to Asherah, similar to the sacred acacia trees dedicated to Iusaaset in Egypt. Iusaaset was the wife of Atum, the Egyptian creator god of Heliopolis that served as the basis of Moses' creator god, and Egyptian equivalent of Ba'al Shalim, the Canaanite god that Jerusalem was named after.

6 Codex Vaticanus: Chousarsathaem (ⲭⲟⲩⲥⲁⲣⲥⲁⲑⲁⲓⲙ)

- Codex Alexandrinus: Chousarsathôm (ⲭⲟⲩⲥⲁⲣⲥⲁⲑⲱⲙ)

- Aleppo Codex: kwšn ršôtym (כושן רשעתים)

- Leningrad Codex: kushan rish'atayim (כּוּשַׁן רִשְׁעָתַיִם)

- Targum Jerusalem: Kushan chayava (כּוּשַׁן חַיָּבָא).

Translation: Kushan sinner (or debtor, stammerer, legal heir)

While the Hebrew term Kush (כוש) referred to the land of Kush, south of Egypt, whose people were known as the Kushi (כּוּשִׁי), Kushan (כּוּשַׁן) was a different term, which the Greeks did not recognize, and therefore transliterated as Chousa (Χουσα). As the term referred to someone who was the king in thee rivers of Aram (Syria), the origin of the word was almost certainly Kasium (𒆳𒆳𒌑𒐉), today translated as Kassite. The Kassites were the rulers of Babylonia in the late bronze age from some time in the 1500s BC, until 1155 BC, when they were conquered by the Elamites. The Hebrew term rishatayim (רִשְׁעָתַיִם) is not proper Hebrew, Canaanite, or Aramaic, however, may be a corruption of the term resha'im (רְשָׁעִים), meaning 'criminals.' Alternatively, this may be the ancient Canaanite spelling of the name of king Paarshataar (𒉺𒊮𒂍𒀭𒊮), more commonly transliterated as Barattarna today, king of the Mitanni Empire circa 1485 BC. Barattarna is recorded as occupying northern Canaan during the reign of Hatshepsut by establishing a series of puppet states across the region, and gaining access to the Mediterranean Sea.

In circa 1479 BC, the Egyptian king Thutmose II died, and his former queen Hatshepsut seized the throne in the name of his two year old son Thutmose III. Hatshepsut was not the mother of Thutmose III, another wife Iset was, whom Hatshepsut married after officially changing her sex to male. After changing genders Hatshepsut declared himself to be Thutmose III's regent, although later assumed the role of king himself until his death, when Thutmose III inherited the throne. While Hatshepsut was a very unpopular king, his rule established the dominant architectural style of the New Kingdom. The entire concept of a female king was rejected by many, with graffiti mocking King Hatshepsut's gender appearing in archaeological records of the era. Most of Kush appears to have rejected Hatshepsut, and rebelled against his rule. After inheriting the throne in circa 1458 BC, Thutmose III attempted to erase Hatshepsut's rule from Egyptian records, claiming to have ruled continuously from the death of Thutmose II in circa 1479 BC. While her role as queen of Thutmose II was never erased, the era when Hatshepsut ruled Egypt was, and his era as king was not rediscovered until the 1800s.

It is clear that there was a rebellion against King Hatshepsut in Syria, backed by the Mitanni, and control of all territory north of Megiddo was lost, as the first thing Thutmose III did after assuming the throne was march north into Canaan, where he fought the battle of Megiddo against the rebelling Syrian kings, and their Mitanni allies. The Battle of Megiddo was the largest battle recorded in Egyptian records up until that time, with both the Egyptians and Canaanite rebels estimated to have fielded around 1,000 chariots and 10,000 infantry. After defeating the Canaanites in the initial battle, the Egyptians plundered 924 chariots and 200 suits of armor. The Canaanite kings fell back to the fortified city of Kadesh, which the Egyptians then besieged for seven months. According to the records at Karnak, when the city surrendered the Egyptians captured 340 Canaanite and Mitanni princes, 2,041 mares, 191 foals, 6 stallions, 924 chariots, 200 suits of armor, 502 bows, 1,929 cattle, and 22,500 sheep.

Between 1458 and 1425 BC, Thutmose III fought a series of campaigns in Canaan, pushing Egyptian control north to the Euphrates River, and then crossed it into the Mitanni empire, where he plundered the country, which apparently had not rebuilt its defenses after the loss at Megiddo. After securing Canaan, Thutmose III marched his army south into Nubia, recapturing territory as far as the fourth cataract, all of which had been lost under the rule of Hatshepsut.

It is unclear why the author would have referred to Barattarna as a Kassite unless it was actually written at the time. The Mitanni rulers are often linked to the Kassites culturally, however, the peoples they ruled were not culturally similar. During the wars of Thutmose III in Canaan, the term Mitanni become common, however, earlier records simply called the land Naharin, meaning 'Rivers,' and called the people Hurrians. While the Hurrians were the primary population of the Mitanni Empire, the rulers were an unrelated group of Indo-Aryans, who spoke a language similar to Sanskrit, and worshiped the Vedic gods. They appear to have seized power over the Hurrians in the Khabur river region in the 1550s BC, from which they expanded in every direction until the Battle of Megiddo.

The Mitanni relationship with the Kassites is unclear, as the Kassites are not viewed as being Indo-Aryans, however, may have been Hurrians. The two cultures were close at the time, and it is plausible that the earliest Mitanni to arrive in the region were viewed as being Kassites by the Canaanites. Nevertheless, by 1457 BC the term would have already been anachronistic, as the term Mitanni would have replaced it, suggesting this verse was written between 1472 and 1457 BC. As the actions of King Barattarna correlate with what Rishatayim is described as doing in the verse, his name is used in this translation, however, it is plausible it was simply a reference to the rebels.

7 Codex Vaticanus: basileôs Syrias potamôn (ΒΑΣΙΛΕΩΣ ΣΥΡΙΑΣΠΟΤΑΜΩΝ). Translation: king of the Syrian rivers

• Aleppo Codex: mlk Årm nhrym (מלך ארס נהרים).
Translation: king of Aram's rivers

• Leningrad Codex: melech Aram naharayim (מֶלֶךְ אֲרַם
נַהֲרַיִם). Translation: king of Aram's rivers

• Targum Jerusalem: malka da'Aram di al Perat (מַלְכָּא דַאֲרָם
דִי עַל פְּרָת). Translation: king of Aram (or Syria) on the Euphrates

The region in question is northern-most modern Syria, and south-east Turkey north of Syria, which was occupied by the Egyptians between 1505 and 1480 BC, and again between 1457 and 1350 BC. The Egyptian name was Naharin, which had been adopted from the local Aramaic word meaning 'rivers.' At the time specified in the Septuagint's chronology, between 1480 and 1472 BC, this was the Mitanni king Barattarna.

8 Codex Vaticanus: Eglôm anêr astios sphodra (ЄΓⲰⲘ ⲀⲚⲎⲢ ⲀⲤⲦⲈⲒⲞⲤ ⲤⲪⲞⲆⲢⲀ). Translation: Elgom was a very handsome (or cosmopolitan, elegant) man

• Aleppo Codex: ôglwn åyš bryå måd (עֶגְלוֹן אִישׁ בָּרִיא מְאֹד). Translation: Eglon was a very healthy (or very fat, lusty) man

• Leningrad Codex: Fglovn ish bari me'od (עֶגְלוֹן אִישׁ בָּרִיא מְאֹד). Translation: Eglon was a very healthy (or very fat, lusty) man

• Targum Jerusalem: Eglon gevar fatim lachada (עֶגְלוֹן גְּבַר פַּטִים לְחֲדָא). Translation: Eglon was a powerful (or strong) perfumed (or fat) one

The Greeks appear to have translated fat (בָּרִיא) as handsome (αστειος) assuming this was a homosexual encounter, however, the Hebrew term implies the man was either healthy or fat or lusty, and later he is confirmed as being very fat.

9 Codex Vaticanus: Setirōtha (ϲⲉⲧⲓⲣⲱⲉⲁ)

• Codex Alexandrinus: Sirōtha (ϲⲉⲓⲣⲱⲉⲁ)

• Aleppo Codex: Šôyrth (שעירתה)

• Leningrad Codex: Se'iratah (שְׂעִירָתָה)

• Targum Jerusalem: Se'irata (שְׂעִירָתָא)

The Greek and Hebrew names appear to be transliterations of the same name, assumed to be an ancient town in the mountains of Ephraim.

Judges: Chapter 4

The Israelites continued to do evil against the Lord after Ehud was dead. The Lord sold the Israelites into the hand of Jabin the king of Canaan who ruled from Hazor,[1] and the chief of the army was Siazara,[2] who lived in the Forge-of-the-Foreigners.[3] The Israelites cried to the Lord because he had nine hundred iron chariots, and he mightily oppressed Israel twenty years. Deborah was a prophetess and the wife of Lapidoth who judged Israel at that time. She sat under the Palm Tree of Deborah between Ramah[4] and Bethel in the mountains of Ephraim, and the Israelites went up to her for judgment.

Deborah sent and called Barak the son of Abinoam out of Kadesh Naphtali, and she asked him, "Has not the Lord God of Israel commanded you, 'Go to Mount Tabor, and take ten thousand men of the Naphtalites and Zebulonites. I will bring to you to the Kishion river, where Siazara the captain of the army of Jabin and his chariots and his multitude are, and I will deliver them into your hands?'"

Barak answered her, "If you will go with me, I will go, and if you will not go, I will not go, as I don't know the day to which the Lord sends his messenger to me."

She replied, "I will certainly go with you, but know that your victory will not depend on the expedition you undertake, for the Lord will sell Siazara into the hands of a woman."

Deborah left Kadesh with Barak. Barak called the Zebulonites and Naphtalites out of Kadesh, and 10,000 men went up with him, and Deborah also went up with him. Eber the blacksmith[5] who remained of the blacksmiths,[6] descended from the sons of Jobab, the son-in-law of Moses,[7] pitched his tent by the oak of the covetous ones, which is near Kedesh. Siazara was told that Barak the son of Abinoam had gone up to Mount Tabor. Siazara summoned all his chariots, nine hundred iron chariots, and all the people with him from the Forge-of-the-Foreigners to the Kishion river.

Deborah said to Barak, "Rise, for this is the day on which the Lord has delivered Siazara into your hand. The Lord will go out before you," and Barak went down from Mount Tabor and 10,000 men with him.

The Lord discomfited Siazara, and all his chariots, and army, with the edge of the sword before Barak, and Siazara fell off his chariot and fled on foot. Barak chased after the chariots and army, to the Forge-of-the-Foreigners, and the whole army of Siazara fell by the edge of the sword, and there was no one left. Siazara fled on foot to the tent of Jael the wife of Eber the blacksmith his friend, for there was peace between Jabin king of

Hazor and the house of Eber the blacksmith. Jael went out to meet Siazara, and said to him, "Turn aside my lord, turn aside to me, don't be afraid."

He turned aside to her into the tent, and she covered him with a mantle. Siazara said to her, "Give me, I beg you, a little water to drink, for I am thirsty," and she opened a jug of milk, and gave it to him drink, and covered him.

Siazara told her, "Stand now by the door of the tent, and it will come to pass if any man comes to you, and asks, 'Is there a man here?' Then answer, 'There is not.'"

Jael the wife of Eber took a tent spike and a hammer in her hands, and went secretly to him and held the spike to his temple and drove it through into the ground, and he collapsed, and darkness fell on him and he died. Barak was chasing Siazara, and Jael went out to meet him, and said to him, "Come, and I will take you to the man who you are looking for."

He went with her and saw Siazara was dead, and the spike was in his temple. So God destroyed Jabin king of Canaan on that day before the Israelites. The hand of the Israelites prevailed more and more against King Jabin of Canaan until they completely destroyed King Jabin of Canaan.

Judges: Chapter 4 Notes

1 Codex Vaticanus: Asôr (ᴧϲⲱⲣ)

- Aleppo Codex: Hṣwr (חצור)

- Leningrad Codex: Chatzovr (חָצֹור)

- Targum Jerusalem: Chatzovr (חָצֹור)

Hazor was a major town north of the Sea of Galilee for thousands of years, from at least 2700 BC to the Greek era. The town was mentioned in the Egyptian Execration Texts from the 1700s BC, the Mari Archive of the 1600s BC, the Annals of Thutmoses III in the 1400s BC, the Amarna Letters of the 1300s, and the Papyrus Anastasi I from the 1200s BC. Between 1800 and 1550 BC, the town was a vassal of the city of Qatna, in modern Syria. Hazor was officially annexed by the New Egyptian Empire in 1457 BC when Pharaoh Thutmose III's armies passed through Canaan en route to Syria, however, continued to be governed by local kings subject to the empire. The Amarna Letters include correspondence between the King of Hazor and Pharaoh Akhenaten, specifically EA227 and EA228, the second one mentioning the name of the King of Hazor as being Abdi-Tirshi of 'Hasura.'

These Letters are broadly dated with the rest as being written between 1350 and 1330 BC. According to the chronology of the Septuagint, the era that Jabin of Hazor ruled the Israelites was 1334 to 1314 BC, implying he was appointed by Smenkhkare, Neferneferuaten, or Tutankhamen in the aftermath of Akhenaten's reign (1351 to

1334 BC), or by Siazara when he claimed the throne. This implies that the Judges Ehud and Shamgar were close to the Egyptian crown during their periods as Judge, which would have taken place during the reigns of Amenhotep II, Thutmose IV, Amenhotep III, and Akhenaten.

2 Codex Vaticanus: Sisara (ϲιϲⲁⲣⲁ)

* Aleppo Codex: Sysrå (סיסרא)

* Leningrad Codex: Sisra (סִיסְרָא)

* Targum Jerusalem: Sisra (סִיסְרָא)

This name appears to have been the Egyptian name Siazårô (⸗𓏤𓆈𓅠𓊃⊙), meaning 'recognized son of Ra,' however, this specific name would have denoted a king from either southern Egypt or Nubia, and Siazara is otherwise unknown from regal records. As Siazara is described as commanding an army with 900 iron chariots, this appears to be the Egyptian army stationed in Canaan. Based on the chronologies in the Septuagint's Exodus, Joshua, and Judges, Siazara would have been the commander of the Egyptian forces in Canaan sometime between 1334 to 1314 BC. Iron weapons and chariots had been introduced by the Hyksos dynasty, and the Egyptians of the New Kingdom did use some iron weapons for their military, however, it is not clear if they were still using iron chariots, or have reverted to bronze chariots. It is not known where they were smithing their iron weapons, however, it was not in Egypt and believed to have been somewhere in Canaan or Nubia. This may have been at Site

200 in the Timna Valley, in southern Israel's Arabah region. Site 200 is an iron smelting site worked by Egyptians during the Egyptian New Kingdom era.

3 Codex Vaticanus: Arisôth tôn ethnôn (ⲀⲢⲓⲤⲱⲐ ⲦⲱⲚ ⲈⲞⲚⲰⲚ). Translation: Arisoth the Nations

- Aleppo Codex: ḥršt hgwym (חרשת הגוים)

- Leningrad Codex: charoshet hagGovyim (חֲרֹשֶׁת הַגּוֹיִם). Translation: the forge of the foreigners

- Targum Jerusalem: tekof kerakkei ammaya (תְּקוֹף כְּרַכֵּי עַמְמַיָא). Translation: fortified (or strong) large city of the commoners (or peoples)

The term govyim (גּוֹיִם), translated as 'tribes' (εθνων) in Greek and 'commoners' (עַמְמַיָא) in the Targum Jerusalem, was originally adopted from the Akkadian name of the Gutium (𒆪𒋾𒌝) tribe who lived in the Zagros mountains during the Akkadian and Neo-Sumerian eras. During the Middle Babylonian era, the setting of Judges, the term began being applied to the Indo-European tribes that entered Mesopotamia from the Zagros mountains, including the Kassites, who seized control of Babylon, and then ruled Babylonia for centuries. The only peoples in Canaan likely to be identified as Gutium were the Hyksos and Mitanni. The Smith of the Gutium is described as being the fortress that Siazara's army was based out of. It seems likely the fortress was inherited from the Hyksos Dynasty which built several fortresses in Canaan.

4 Codex Vaticanus: Rama (ƿⱯⲘⱯ)

- Aleppo Codex: Rmh (רמה)

- Leningrad Codex: Ramah (רָמֶה)

- Targum Jerusalem: Yricho pardesin beramata zeitin avedin meshach bevik'ata beit shakya (יְרִיחוֹ פַּרְדְּסִין בְּרָמָתָא וְזֵיתִין עָבְדִין מְשַׁח בְּבִקְעָתָא בֵּית שָׁקְיָא). Translation: Jericho's orchards (or walled gardens) and Ramah's olives, creators of perfume in the valley of Beth Shakya

A town called Ramah was located near Gibeah in the Book of Joshua.

5 Codex Vaticanus: Chaber o Cinaeos (ⲬⱯⲂⲈƿ ⲞⲔⲒⲚⱯⲒⲞⲤ). Translation: Chaber the Cinaeos

- Codex Alexandrinus: plêsion tou Cinaeou (ⲦⲦⱯⲎⲤⲒⲞⲚ ⲦⲞⲨⲔⲒⲚⱯⲒⲞⲨ). Translation: near the Cinaeou

- Aleppo Codex: Ḥbr ḥqyny (חבר הקיני). Translation: Ḥbr the Kenite (or smith)

- Leningrad Codex: Chever hakkeini (חֶבֶר הַקֵּינִי). Translation: Heber the Kenite (or smith)

- Targum Jerusalem: Chever Shalma'ah (חֶבֶר שַׁלְמָאָה). Translation: Heber Shalmaite

As the term Kenite means blacksmith, he is referred to him as 'Heber the blacksmith' in this translation. The Shalmaites mentioned in the Jerusalem Targum were a tribe of arabs from the late-Classical era, 2000 years after the era the book is set in.

6 Codex Vaticanus: Caena (ΚΑΙΝΑ)

• Codex Alexandrinus: the term is omitted from the verse

• Aleppo Codex: qyn (קין). Translation: smith, metalworker, blacksmith

• Leningrad Codex: kayin (קַיִן). Translation: smith, metalworker, blacksmith

• Targum Jerusalem: Shalma'ei (שַׁלְמָאִי). Translation: Shalmaites

7 Codex Vaticanus: Iôbab gambrou Môysê (ΙΩΒΑΒ ΓΑΜΒΡΟΥΜΩΥCH). Translation: Jobab bridegroom of Moses

• Aleppo Codex: Hbb htn Mšh (חבב חתן משה). Translation: Hbb groom Moses

• Leningrad Codex: Chovav choten Mosheh (חֹבָב חֹתֵן מֹשֶׁה). Translation: Hobab groom Moses

• Targum Jerusalem: Chovav chamuhi deMosheh (חוֹבָב חֲמוּהִי דְמֹשֶׁה). Translation: Hobab in the house of Moses

Judges: Chapter 5

Deborah and Barak ben Abinoam, sang on that day:

A revelation was made in Israel when the people were made willing!

Praise you, Lord!

Listen you kings! Listen governors,[1] and I will sing!

I will sing to the Lord! I will!

I will sing a psalm to the Lord God of Israel!

Lord, in your going out on Seir, when you went out of the land of Edom, the earth quaked and the sky dropped dew, and the cloud rained.

The mountains were shaken before the face of the Lord, the Sinai before the face of the Lord God of Israel.

In the days of Shamgar son of Anath, in the days of Jael, they deserted the ways and became perverse.

The mighty men in Israel failed, they failed until Deborah arose as a mother for Israel.

They chose new gods, then the rulers of cities fought, and there was no shield or spear seen among forty thousand Israelites.

My heart listens to the orders given in Israel, you that are willing among the people, bless the Lord.

You who move as Aten the sun god at midday,[2] sitting in judgment, and following the path, and riding the pathway, declare from the noise of disturbers among the drawers of water and retell the righteous acts of the Lord. Increase righteous acts in Israel, then the people of the Lord will go down to the cities.

Awake, awake, Deborah! Awake, awake, sing a song!

Rise, Barak, and catch captives, son of Abinoam.

Then the survivors went down against the nobles, the people of the Lord went down for him among the mighty ones from me. Ephraim rooted them out in Amalek, then Benjamin with your people from Machir came down with me hunting out the enemy, and from Zebulun came those that write with the scribe's pen to record.

Princes of Issachar were with Deborah and Barak, so she sent Barak on foot into the valley to the portions of Reuben. Great pangs reached the heart.

Why did they sit between the sheepfolds to hear the bleating of flocks for the divisions of Reuben? There was great searching of hearts. Gilead is on the other side of Jordan where he pitched his tents. Why does Dan remain in ships? Asher sat down on the sea-coasts, and he will camp at his ports. The people of Zebulun exposed their mind to death, and Naphtali went to the high places of their land.

Kings set themselves in formation, and then the kings of Canaan fought in Ti'inik at the water of Megiddo, and they took no bribe of money. The stars from the sky set themselves in formation, they left their paths to fight with Siazara. The brook of Kishion swept them away, the ancient brook, the brook Kishion.

"My mighty mind will trample him down. When the hoofs of the horse were entangled, his mighty ones earnestly rushed to curse Southern Egypt.[3] Curse it," said the messenger of the lord, "Cursed is everyone who dwells in it, because they did not come to help the Lord, to help him among the mighty."

"Blessed among women be Jael the wife of Eber the blacksmith. Let her be blessed above women in tents. He asked for water, and she gave him milk in a dish, she brought butter of princes, she stretched out her left hand to the spike, and her right to the hand workman's hammer and she struck Siazara with it, she nailed through his head and murdered him!"

"She nailed through his temples! He rolled down between her feet, and he fell and lay between her feet. He collapsed and fell, where he collapsed, there he fell dead."

"The mother of Siazara looked down through the window out of the loophole, saying, 'Why was his chariot ashamed? Why did the wheels of his chariots wait?'"

"Her wise ladies answered her, and she returned answers to herself, 'Won't they find him dividing the plunder? He will certainly be gracious to every man! There are spoils of dyed garments for Siazara, spoils of various dyed garments, dyed embroidered garments, they are the spoils for his neck.'"

"So let all your enemies perish, Lord! They who love him will be like the sun[4] coming in his strength."

The land had peace for forty years.[5]

Judges: Chapter 5 Notes

1 Codex Vaticanus: satrapae (ϹΑΤΡΑΠΑΙ). Translation: satraps

- Codex Alexandrinus: satrapae dynatoe (ϹΑΤΡΑΠΑΙ ΔΥΝΑΤΟΙ). Translation: satraps of power (or forces)

- Aleppo Codex: {R} rznym {S} ånky ({ר} אנכי {ס} רזנים)

- Leningrad Codex: rozenim anochi (רֹזְנִים אָנֹכִי)

- Targum Jerusalem: shiltonaya (שִׁלְטוֹנַיָא). Translation: sultans

The Greeks substituted the word in the Old Aramaic text as 'satraps,' the Persian word for governors, however, that is not a translation of the term in the Hebrew translation. Likewise, the translator of the Targum Jerusalem substituted 'sultans.' The Aleppo Codex indicates that the terms 'rznym' and 'ånky' were found in two different source texts, however the Leningrad Codex later treats them as continuous string of words. Neither term is actually Hebrew, however, rznym (רזנים) is generally assumed to be scribal error of rbnym (רבנים), meaning 'great ones' which may be the source of the Greek 'satraps,' however, it is more likely that 'satraps' was already added to the Aramaic text the Greeks translated, as they had no reason to substitute a Persian word.

Assuming that rznym is a scribal error of rbnym, this error must have taken place when the cuneiform text of Judges, or possibly just a book of Deborah and Barak was translated into Canaanite. The Akkadian cuneiform BÈ (𒁀) was part of the ZÁ (𒍝), along with the UD (𒌓). As the UD also held the phonetic value of U, it would have simply meant the original Canaanite cuneiform word in the text was a plural of rabbu (𒂍𒄭𒀭), which mirrors the reconstructed pronunciation of the word rabbu (𒂍𒊮), the in Ugaritic Canaanite version of the word from the same era.

None of the other scripts that the book could have been written in had similar letters for B and Z, including Egyptian hieroglyphics as used to spell Canaanite words: B (𓉔) and Z (𓅱), Paleo-Canaanite: B (𐤁) and Z (=), Phoenician Canaanite: B (𐤁) and Z (𐤆), and Aramaic: B (𐡁) and Z (𐡆). The translation of 'satraps of power,' found in the Codex Alexandrinus, indicates that the two words were already in a combined form of the text by the 5th century, and that the Greeks interpreted Ånky (אנכי) as a reference to the Anaki (עֲנָק). The Ånåkj (𓄿𓅱𓄿𓃥) were also recorded in Egyptian records from the Middle Kingdoms as having lived in the region of mount Hermon and mount Carmel, however, they do not appear to have still been around in the New Kingdom era, suggesting it was an attempt to interpret the word rznym after the script had been translated into Proto-Canaanite or Canaanite. As the original term in the text was probably 'rabbu' which is essentially the bronze age version of the Septuagint's 'satrap,' and Targum Jerusalem's 'sultan,' the term 'governor' is used in this translation.

2 Codex Vaticanus: epibebêcotes epi onou thêlias mesêmbrias cathêmenoe epi critêriou cae poreuomenoe epi odous synedrôn eph odô (ΕΠΙΒΕΒΗΚΟΤΕϹ ΕΠΙ ΟΝΟΥ

ΘΗΛΕΙΑϹ ΜΕϹΗΜΒΡΙΑϹ ΚΑΘΗΜΕΝΟΙ ΕΠΙ ΚΡΙΤΗΡΙΟΥ ΚΑΙ ΠΟΡΕΥΟΜΕΝΟΙ ΕΠΙ ΟΔΟΥϹ ϹΥΝΕΔΡΩΝ ΕΦ ΟΔΩ). Translation: "You who rides on a single female at noon, sitting in judgment, and following the path, and riding the pathway."

• Codex Alexandrinus: epibebêcotes epi ypozygiôn cathêmenoe epi lampênôn (ΕΠΙΒΕΒΗΚΟΤΕϹ ΕΠΙ ΥΠΟΖΥΓΙΩΝ ΚΑΘΗΜΕΝΟΙ ΕΠΙ ΛΑΜΠΠΗΝΩΝ). Translation: "You who ride on a beast of burden and covered chariots."

• Aleppo Codex: rkby åtnwt shrwt {s} yšby {r} ôl mdyn whlky ôl drk--šyhw {s} (רכבי אתנות צחרות {ס} ישבי {ר} על מדין {ס} והלכי על דרך--שיחו {ס}). Translation: "You who mount tribes [S] inhabitants [R] in Midian and travel along the path, speak [S]"

• Leningrad Codex: rochevei atonovt tzechorovt yoshevei al-middin veholechei al-derech sichu (רֹכְבֵי אֲתֹנוֹת צְחֹרוֹת יֹשְׁבֵי עַל־מִדִּין וְהֹלְכֵי עַל־דֶּרֶךְ שִׂיחוּ). Translation: "You who ride on white donkeys, and sit in Midian and travel along the path, speak."

The verse had been a mystery for thousands of years, as God should not be described as riding a 'female at noon,' 'beasts of burden and covered chariots,' or 'white donkeys.' Åtnwt (אתנות) appears to be an ancient attempt to transliterate Aten (𒀭𒌋 ⊙) into Aramaic and then Hebrew via the Akkadian Cuneiform Iaati anUtu (𒂍𒄿𒆷𒀭𒌋), meaning 'Aten god of the Sun.' This would mean the verse was something like:

"You who move as Aten the sun god at midday, sitting in judgment, and following the path, and riding the pathway."

Aten was the Egyptian solar-god during the reign of Akhenaten (1353 to 1336 BC), whose name translates in Egyptian as 'disk.' The name Aten fell out of use in Egypt during the restoration of the old gods by Pharaoh Horemheb (1319-1292 BC), implying the Song of Deborah and Barak date to before the end of this era. Based on the dating of the Book of Judges found in the Septuagint, the song would have been sung in 1314 BC, five years into Horemheb's reign.

3 Codex Vaticanus: Mêrôz (ΜΗΡѠΖ)

- Codex Alexandrinus: Marôz (ΜΑΡѠΖ)

- Aleppo Codex: Mrwz (מרוז)

- Leningrad Codex: Meroz (מֵרוֹז)

- Targum Jerusalem: Meroz (מֵרוֹז)

Interpretations of what Merez was, differ wildly. Some associate it with the village of Mitzr (כְּפָר מִצָר) in northern Israel, southwest of the Sea of Galilee. The Village of Misr was founded at some point by Egyptian settlers in Canaan, however, it is unclear when. The oldest ruins discovered in the village only date back to the Roman era, however, the name is Arabic, indicating that this community was founded long after the time of Deborah.

A commentary in the Talmud (Moed Katan 16a) claims that Meroz is a planet that refused to help the Israelites in their time of trouble, however, the name Meroz does not correlate with the Canaanite name of any planet. The author of Moed Katan was probably conflating the Hebrew word from Judges with the Roman name Mars, which would have been anachronistic, as even if a precursor to the Latin language existed in the late Bronze Age, there is no reason an Israelite would have used the proto-Latin name.

None of the known variants of the Semitic name of Egypt are a close match to Meroz/Maroz, however, the Egyptian name Marēs, is almost phonetically identical. Mâôresi (⌣ ⌐ 𝄃) was an ancient Egyptian name for Southern Egypt, which translates as approximately 'Southern Place.' It continued to be used until the Classical era, when it was pronounced as Marēs (Μαρнс). The exact pronunciation of ancient Egyptian names is debated before the development of the Demotic script, and therefore it cannot be known how the Egyptians pronounced Maaresi during the era of Deborah, however, it is documented in Late Egyptian Demotic as being Mâôrs ('ʾ/ʾƷ͡ɔ), supporting the New Kingdom era pronunciation as being very similar to the term used by Deborah.

The simplest explanation is that the word Mrwz (מרוז) referred to Southern Egypt itself, and not the village named 'Egypt.' At the time, the Egyptian imperial capital was in Thebes, the capital of Southern Egypt. Therefore, the implication is that King Jabin and the Egyptian General Siazara, were rebelling against Egypt, and the Egyptians did not send relief into Canaan to help their subjects. As the

Septuagint dates their rule over Canaan to between 1334 and 1314 BC, this means they seized control when Akenhaten died, and ruled throughout the brief reigns of Smenkhkare (1335-1334 BC), Neferneferuaten (1334-1332 BC), Tutankhamen (1334-1325 BC), and Ay (1332-1319 BC), as well as the first five years of Horemheb (1319-1292 BC). This was a chaotic period in Egyptian history, and it is possible the entire Egyptian army in Canaan rebelled, as it wasn't entirely clear who the Pharaoh actually was during most of this period. General Siazara may have not seen his army as being in rebellion if he did not see the government in Egypt as valid.

By year five of Horemheb's reign, it would have been clear that the government had been restored in Egypt, and his position in Canaan would have become a clear case of rebellion, which would explain why his army had become so ineffective as his troops abandoned him to return to Egypt. As the word does appear to be s reference to Southern Egypt, that name is restored in this translation.

4 Codex Vaticanus: Êliou (ΗΛΙΟΥ). Translation: Helios

• Codex Alexandrinus: tou Êliou (ΤΟΥΗΛΙΟΥ). Translation: the sun

• Aleppo Codex: hšmš (הֺשׁמשׁ). Translation: the sun

• Leningrad Codex: hashemesh (הַשֶּׁמֶשׁ). Translation: the sun

• Targum Jerusalem: shimsha (שִׁמְשָׁא). Translation: sun

Shemesh was the Canaanite sun god, whose worship was later banned by King Josiah. The presence of a sun-god in the text supports the earlier reading of åtnwt (אתנות) as Aten, as Aten was the dominant Egyptian solar-god at the time, and Canaan was part of the Egyptian Empire at the time.

5 Based on the chronology of the Septuagint, these forty years of peace ended in 1279 BC, when Ramesses II launched his first campaign against Syria.

Judges: Chapter 6

The Israelites did evil in the sight of the Lord, and the Lord gave them into the hand of Midian for seven years. The hand of Midian prevailed against Israel, and the Israelites made for themselves the caves in the mountains, and the dens, and the holes in the rocks because of Midian. It happened when the Israelites sowed, that the Midianites, Amalekites, and Nesites[1] went up together. They camped against them and destroyed their fruits as far as Gaza, and they did not leave the support of life in the land of Israel, and not even an ox or donkey among the herds. They brought their animals and came with their tents in great numbers like the locusts, and there was no counting them and their camels. They came to the land of Israel and laid waste to it.

Israel was greatly impoverished because of Midian and the Israelites cried to the Lord because of Midian. The Lord sent a prophet to the Israelites, and he said to them, "The Lord God of Israel says, 'I am he who brought you up out of the land of Egypt, and I brought you up out of the house of your slavery. I delivered you out of the hands of Egypt, and out of the hands of all that attacked you, and I drove them out before you, and I gave you their land. I said to you, 'I am the Lord God, you will not fear the gods of the Amorites in whose land you live,' but you did not listen to my voice."

The messenger of the lord came and sat down under the fir tree, which was in Ephrath in the land of Joash the father of Esdri. Gideon his son was threshing wheat in a wine press to escape from the face of Midian. The messenger of the lord appeared to him and said to him, "The Lord is with you, and you are mighty in strength."

Gideon replied to him, "Be gracious with me, my lord, but if the Lord is with us, why have these evils found us? Where are all his miracles, which our fathers have told us about, when they said, 'Did not the Lord bring us up out of Egypt?' Now he has abandoned us and given us into the hand of Midian."

The messenger of the lord turned to him and said, "Go in your strength, and you will save Israel out of the hand of Midian. Look, I have sent you."

Gideon asked him, "Be gracious with me, my lord. How will I save Israel? Look, my thousand[2] are weak among Manasseh, and I am the least in my father's house."

The messenger of the lord answered him, "The Lord will be with you, and you will slaughter Midian like one man."

Gideon said to him, "If I have found mercy in your eyes, and you will do for me all that you have said to me today, don't leave here until I come to you, and I will bring an offering and offer it to you."

He replied, "I will remain until you return."

Gideon went and prepared a goat-kid and a bushel of fine unleavened flour, and he put the meat in the basket, and poured the broth into the pot, and brought them out to him under the turpentine tree, and approached.

The messenger of God said to him, "Take the meat and the unleavened cakes, and put them on that rock, and pour out the broth nearby," and he did so. The messenger of the lord stretched out the end of the wand that was in his hand and touched the flesh and the unleavened bread, and fire came up out of the rock and consumed the flesh and the unleavened bread, and the messenger of the lord vanished from his sight.

Gideon understood that he was the messenger of the lord, and Gideon said, "Oh my Lord God! I have seen the messenger of the lord face to face!"

The Lord said to him, "Peace be to you, and don't be afraid, as you will not die."

Gideon built an altar there to the Lord, and called it Lord Shalim.[3] Until this day, as it is still in Ephrath of the father of Esdri. It happened that night, that the Lord said to him, "Take the young bull which your father has, the second bull which is seven years old, and destroy the altar of Ba'al which your father has, and the Asherah which is by it, you will also destroy. You will build an altar to the Lord God on the top of the rocky mountain[4] in the appointed place, and you will take the second bull and will offer up whole burnt offerings with the wood of the grove, which you will destroy."

Gideon took ten men from his servants and did as the Lord had told him, and as he was afraid of what the house of his father and the men of the city would do if he did it in the daytime, so he did it at night. The men of the city rose up early in the morning and saw the altar of Ba'al had been demolished, and the Asherah next to it had been destroyed, and they saw the second bull which Gideon offered on the altar that had been built. Men asked their neighbors, "Who has done this?" and they inquired and searched, and learned that Gideon the son of Joash had done this thing.

The men of the city demanded of Joash, "Bring out your son, and let him die because he has destroyed the altar of Ba'al and because he has destroyed the Asherah that was by it."

Gideon the son of Joash said to all the men who rose up against him, "Do you now plead for Ba'al? Will you save him? Whoever will plead for him, let him be murdered this morning! If he is a god, let him plead for himself, because someone has torn down his altar."

He called it on that day Jerubbaal, saying, "Let Ba'al plead because his altar has been overthrown."

All Midian and Amalek, and the Nesites themselves together and camped in the valley of Jezreel.[5] The wind of the Lord came on Gideon, and he blew with the horn, and Abiezer came to follow him. Gideon sent messengers to all Manasseh, Asher, and Zebulun, and Naphtali, and he went up to meet them. Gideon said to God, "If you will save Israel by my hand, as you have promised, I have put the fleece of wool in the threshing floor, and if there is dew on the fleece only, and the rest of the ground is dry, I will know that you will save Israel by my hand, as you have said."

It was so, and he rose up early in the morning and wrung the fleece, and dew dropped from the fleece, filling a full bowl of water.

Gideon said to God, "I beg you, don't become angry with me, and I will speak again. I will   make one more test with the fleece. Let the fleece only be dry, and let there be dew on all the ground."

God made it so that night, and only the fleece was dry, and on all the ground there was dew.

Judges: Chapter 6 Notes

1 Codex Vaticanus: uioe anatolôn (ΥΙΟΙΑΝΑΤΟΛΩΝ). Translation: sons of the east

- Aleppo Codex: bny qdm (בני קדם). Translation: sons of the east (or ancients)

- Leningrad Codex: venei-kedem (בְנֵי-קֶדֶם). Translation: sons of the east (or ancients)

- Dead Sea Scroll 4QJudgᵃ: bny qdm (בגי קדם). Translation: sons of the east (or ancients)

- Targum Jerusalem: venei madincha (בְּנֵי מַדִינְחָא). Translation: sons of the country (or city, Medina)

The 'East' in ancient Canaan referred to Mesopotamia, meaning that the Israelites were referring to a Mesopotamian people plundering the land with the support of the Midianites and Amalekites. The Septuagint's chronology places this 7-year period in approximately 1274 to 1267 BC. This time period corresponds to Ramesses II's campaigns in Canaan against the Nesites (𓉔𓈖𓇋𓊃𓏏), often misidentified as Hittites, between 1274 and 1269 BC. By Ramesses II's reign, the Egyptians had lost control of northern Canaan to the Nesites, and in 1274 BC Ramesses launched an invasion of northern Canaan, attempting to recapture Kadesh. The first campaign, in 1274 BC, was a failure, although Egypt did weaken the Nesite army in the south. The second campaign, in 1273 BC, was also a failure, although the Egyptians did reach the outskirts of Kadesh. The third campaign, in 1271 BC, successfully captured Kadesh, and pushed the Nesites out of Canaan. In the following years, Egypt consolidated control over Canaan, occupying Edom, Seir, Moab, Jerusalem, Jericho, Heshbon, and Damascus, most of which submitted to Egypt peacefully. This consolidation of Egyptian authority in Canaan is believed to have only taken until 1269 BC according to Egyptologists, however, the Book of Judges reports it took until 1267 BC. The conflict with the Nesites did continue after 1269 BC, and the peace treaty between Egypt and the Nesites was not signed until 1258 BC. This indicates the people referred to in Judges as 'sons of the East,' were Nesites, which is the term used in this translation.

2 Codex Vaticanus: chilias (ΧΙΛΙΑC). Translation: thousand

- Aleppo Codex: âlpy (אלפי). Translation: thousands

- Leningrad Codex: alpi (אַלְפִּי). Translation: thousands

- Targum Jerusalem: zar'iti (זַרְעִיתִי). Translation: families

3 Codex Vaticanus: eirênê cu (ΕΙΡΗΝΗ‾Κ‾Υ‾). Translation: peace lord

- Aleppo Codex: Yhwh šlwm (יהוה שלום). Translation: Yhwh peace (or Shalim)

- Leningrad Codex: Yehvah shalovm (יְהוָה שָׁלוֹם). Translation: Yehwah peace

JUDGES: CHAPTER 6 NOTES

• Targum Jerusalem: Yeyah da'avad leih shelam (יְיָ דַּעֲבַד לֵיהּ שְׁלָם). Translation: Yahw serves the Yah to be complete (or to be Shalim, until evening)

As the Greek translation predates the Hasmonean redaction of circa 140 BC that inserted Yehvah, it reads 'Lord' instead of Yehvah. The Aramaic version of Judges likely read ådny šlmå (אֲדֹנָי שְׁלָם), meaning 'Lord Peace,' which was both the Greek translation and the Masoretic interpretation of the Hebrew translation. The Hebrew term šlwm (שְׁלוֹם) is a transliteration of the Phoenician term šlm (𐤔𐤋𐤌), which can be translated as either 'peace' or 'Shalim,' the name of the god of the evening, known as Atum in Egyptian, and the name of the god that Jerusalem was named after. As Shalim was one of the ancient Canaanite Lords at the time, it is likely that the earlier Phoenician text read Ba'al Shalim (𐤔𐤋𐤌 𐤁𐤏𐤋). The Hasmoneans redacted most instances of Adon and Ba'al to Yehvah around 140 BC, resulting in the strange expression 'Yehvah Peace' in the Masoretic Text, however, there is no evidence of a community named after 'Yehvah Peace' in Canaan in the 1200s BC.

4 Codex Vaticanus: Maouec (ΜΑΟΥΕΚ)

• Codex Alexandrinus: Maôz (ΜΑΩΖ)

• Aleppo Codex: môwz (מעוז). Translation: rock (or stone)

• Leningrad Codex: ma'ovz (מָעוֹז). Translation: rock (or stone)

- Targum Jerusalem: tukefa (תּוּקְפָא). Translation: power

The Greeks transliterated the Aramaic word for 'rock' which is used in this translation.

5 Codex Vaticanus: Ezereel (ε ζ ε ρ ε ε λ)

- Codex Alexandrinus: Iezrael (ι ε ζ ρ α ε λ)

- Aleppo Codex: Yzrôål (יזרעאל)

- Leningrad Codex: Yizre'el (יִזְרְעֶאל)

- Targum Jerusalem: Yizre'el (יִזְרְעֶאל)

The Jazreel Valley is in northern Israel and was along the over land route between Egypt and Syria. Some scholars believe the name Jezreel was the origin of the name Israel, as the valley runs through ancient Samaria. If the Nesites pushed as far south as Jazreel, it would have likely been between Ramesses II's first Syrian campaign in 1273 BC, and the Battle of Kadesh in 1269 BC when Ramesses II pushed the Nesites out of Canaan.

Judges: Chapter 7

Jerubbaal rose early, as did Gideon and all the people with him, and camped at the Fountain of Arad. The camp of Midian was to the north of him, reaching from the Hill of Moreh, in the valley.

The Lord said to Gideon, "The people with you are many, so many that I may not deliver Midian into their hand, in case at any time Israel boasts against me, saying, 'My own hand has saved me.' Now tell the people, 'Whoever is afraid and fearful? Let him turn and leave Mount Gilead,'" and twenty-two thousand people left, leaving ten thousand.

The Lord said to Gideon, "The people are still too numerous, bring them down to the water, and I will purge them there for you. It will happen that whoever I will say to you, 'This one will go with you,' he will go with you, and of whoever I will say to you, 'This one will not go with you,' he will not go with you."

He brought the people down to the water, and the Lord said to Gideon, "Whoever will lap of the water with his tongue like a dog, you will set him apart, and also whoever will kneel on his knees to drink."

The count of those that lapped with their hand to their mouth was three hundred men, and all the rest of the people knelled on their knees to drink water. The Lord said to Gideon, "I will save you by the three hundred men that lapped, and I will give Midian into your hand, and all the rest of the people will go everyone to his home."

They took the provisions of the people in their hands and their horns, and he sent away every man of Israel each to his tent, and he strengthened the three hundred, and the army of Midian was beneath him in the valley. In that night the Lord said to him, "Rise, go down into the camp, for I have delivered it into your hand. If you are afraid to go down, go down with Pharaoh's servant[1] to the soldiers' camp. You will hear what they will say, and afterward, your hands will be strong, and you will go down into the camp."

He and Pharaoh's servant went down to the extremity of the companies of fifty, which were in the camp. Midian and Amalek and all the Nesites were scattered in the valley like locusts in multitude, and there was no counting their camels, and they were like the sand of the seashore for multitude. Gideon came and heard a man describing a dream to his neighbor. He said, "Look, I have dreamed a dream, in which a cake of barley bread rolled into the camp of Midian, and it came as far as a tent and hit it, and it fell, and it turned over, and the tent fell."

His neighbor replied, "This is none other than the sword of Gideon, son of Joash, an Israelite. God has delivered Midian and all the army into his hand."

When Gideon heard the account of the dream and the interpretation of it, he worshiped the Lord and returned to the camp of Israel, and said, "Rise, for the Lord has delivered the camp of Midian into our hand."

He divided the three hundred men into three companies and put horns in the hands of all, and empty pitchers, and torches in the pitchers, and he said to them, "You will watch me, and this is what you will do. I will go into the army, and as I do, you will also do. I will blow with the horn, and all you with me will blow with the horn around the whole camp, and you will shout, "For the Lord and Gideon."

Gideon and the hundred men that were with him came to the outskirts of the army at the beginning of the midnight watch, and they completely roused the guards and sounded with the horns, and they broke the pitchers that were in their hands, and the three companies sounded with the horns, and broke the pitchers, and held the torches in their left hands, and in their right hands their horns to sound with. They cried out, "A sword for the Lord and Gideon."

Every man stood in his place around the army, and all the army ran, and sounded an alarm, and fled. They sounded with the three hundred horns, and the Lord set every man's sword in all the army against his neighbor. The army fled as far as the Temple of Seth in Garagatha,[2] Abel-meholah,[3] and Tabbath, and the Israelites from Naphtali, Asher, and Manasseh came to help and chased after Midian. Gideon sent messengers into all the mountains of Ephraim, saying, "Come down to meet Midian, and capture for yourselves the water as far as the House of Barah on the Jordan."

Every Ephraimite cried out, and they captured the water all the way to the House of Barah on the Jordan. They captured the princes of Midian, including Oreb and Zeeb. They killed Oreb in Sur Oreb, and killed Zeeb at the winepress of Zeeb,[4] and they crushed Midian and brought the heads of Oreb and Zeeb to Gideon from beyond the Jordan.

Judges: Chapter 7 Notes

1 Codex Vaticanus: Phara to paedarion (ΦΑΡΑΤΟ ΠΑΙΔΑΡΙΟΝ). Translation: Phara the child (or servant)

• Aleppo Codex: prh nôrk (פרה נערך). Possible translation: carrying (or cow, Purah) boy (or servant, youth)

• Leningrad Codex: furah na'archa (פֻרָה נַעֲרֶךָ). Possible translation: carrying (or cow, Purah) boy (or servant, youth)

• Targum Jerusalem: furah ulemach (פּוּרָה עוּלֵמָךְ). Translation: framework (or wine press) the world

Based on the context, this strange sentence appears to be a reverence to an Egyptian overseer stationed by Pharaoh among the Tribe of Manasseh. The Phoenician spelling of 'pharaoh' was prôh (𐤐𐤓𐤏), while the Aramaic spelling was prôwn (פרעון), neither of which is an exact match for the transliterated words prh (פרה) and phara (φαρα), indicating that neither the Paleo-Hebrew nor Aramaic texts included the word 'pharaoh' but a similar sounding word. This suggests that the word, along with the Song of Deborah, was transliterated from another script, likely Akkadian Cuneiform or Egyptian.

The Akkadian Cuneiform spelling of 'pharaoh' was pirôû (𒉿𒊒𒌑) during the late Bronze Age, while the Egyptian spelling was pr-ôå (𓉐𓂋𓉻) during the late Bronze era and early Iron Age. While either script could have been used at the time, the cuneiform name is pronounced almost exactly like the term found in the Hebrew translation, while the

Egyptian is pronounced slightly differently, suggesting the original text was in cuneiform.

2 Codex Vaticanus: Bêthseedta Garagatha (ʙʜⲟⲥⲉⲉⲇⲧⲁ ⲅⲁⲣⲁⲅⲁⲑⲁ)

• Codex Alexandrinus: Baethasetta (ʙⲁⲓⲟⲁⲥⲉⲧⲧⲁ)

• Aleppo Codex: byt hšth ṣrrth (בית השטה צררתה)

• Leningrad Codex: beit hashittah tzereratah (בֵּית הַשִּׁטָּה צְרֵרָתָה)

• Targum Jerusalem: beit shitah litzreirat (בֵּית שִׁיטָה לְצְרֵירַת)

The term vyt hoshth (בית השטה) translates as House of 'sth,' which appears to be a transliterated name, possibly Seth, the Egyptian god that had been widely worshiped by the Hyksos. Shth (שטה) could also be a spelling error of shvth (שוטה), meaning 'fool,' or shyth (שיטה), meaning 'system.' As Seth is a direct translation, the term 'House of Seth in Garagatha,' is used. Zererah is spelled in various ways in the Masoretic Text and transliterated in various ways, including Zaretan, Zarethan, Zeredathah, Zartanah, or Zarthan. It is believed the town was in the Jordan valley, south of the Sea of Galilee. It is unclear if Garagatha was an alternate name for Zererah or another location, however, as the names are noticeably different the Greek term is used.

3 Codex Vaticanus: Abômeoula (ΑΒѠΜΕΟΥΛΛ)

- Codex Alexandrinus: Abelmeoula (ΑΒΕΛΜΕΟΥΛΛ)

- Aleppo Codex: Åbl mhwlh (**אבל מחולה**)

- Leningrad Codex: Avel mechovlah (אָבֵל מְחוֹלָה)

- Targum Jerusalem: Avel mechovlah (אָבֵל מְחוֹלָה)

Abel-meholah would later be the birth town of the prophet Elisha. It was described as being near the Jordan River, south of the House of She'an (Beit She'an), which would seem to confirm that Zererah was somewhere in the area.

4 Codex Vaticanus: Iacephzêph (ΙΛΚΕΦΖΗΦ)

- Codex Alexandrinus: Iacephzêb (ΙΛΚΕΦΖΗΒ)

- Aleppo Codex: byqb zåb (**ביקב זאב**). Translation: wine press of Zeeb

- Leningrad Codex: vcyekev-Ze'ev (בְיָקֶב-זְאֵב). Translation: wine press of Zeeb

- Targum Jerusalem: meishar Ze'ev (מֵישַׁר זְאֵב). Translation: level (or upright) of Zeeb

As the Greeks transliterated the word 'wine press of Zeeb' as Ιακεφζηφ or Ιακεφζηβ, the Hebrew translation is imported from the Masoretic Text.

Judges: Chapter 8

The Ephraimites said to Gideon, "What is this that you have done to us, in that you did not call us when you went to fight with Midian?"

They rebuked him sharply, and later when their spirit calmed towards him, he replied to them, "What have I now done in comparison to you? Is not the gleaning of Ephraim better than the vintage of Abiezer? The Lord has delivered into your hand the princes of Midian, both Oreb and Zeeb, and what could I do in comparison to you?"

Gideon came to Jordan, and went over, himself and the three hundred with him, hungry, yet still chasing. He said to the men of Succoth, "Give, I beg you, bread to feed these people that follow me, because they are tired, and look, I am chasing after Zebah and Zalmunna, the kings of Midian."

The princes of Succoth asked, "Are the hands of Zebah and Zalmunna now in your hand, that we should give bread to your army?"

Gideon answered, "When the Lord gives Zebah and Zalmunna into my hand, then I will scourge your flesh with the thorns of the wilderness, and briers.

He went up from there to Penuel and spoke to them the same way, and the men of Penuel answered him as the men of Succoth had answered him. Gideon said to the men of Penuel, "When I return in victory, I will break down this tower."

Zebah and Zalmunna were in Karkor, and their army was with them, about fifteen thousand, all that were left of the army of the Neshites,[1] and they that fell were a hundred and twenty thousand men that drew the sword. Gideon went up by the way of them that lived in tents, east of Nobah and Jogbehah, and he struck the army, and the army was secure. Zebah and Zalmunna fled, and he chased after them, and took the two kings of Midian, Zebah, and Zalmunna, and discomfited all the army.

Gideon the son of Joash returned from the battle, from the Ascent of Heres.[2] He took as prisoner a boy from Succoth and questioned him, and he wrote for him the names of the princes of Succoth and their elders, seventy-seven men. Gideon came to the princes of Succoth, and said, "Look Zebah and Zalmunna, who you teased me about, saying, 'Are the hands of Zebah and Zalmunna now in your hand, that we should give bread to your men that are faint?'"

He took the elders of the city and he scourged them with the thorns of the wilderness and the briers. He torn down the tower of Penuel and killed the men of the city. He asked Zebah and Zalmunna, "Where are the men who you killed in Tabor?"

They answered, "Like you, they were in the ranks of the sons of the king."[3]

Gideon said, "They were my brothers and the sons of my mother. As the Lord lives, if you had kept them alive, I would not murder you."

He said to Jetheth his firstborn, "Rise and kill them," but the boy did not draw his sword, for he was afraid, as he was still very young.

Zebah and Zalmunna said, "Rise and attack us, for your strength is like that of a man," and Gideon rose, and killed Zebah and Zalmunna, and he took the round ornaments that were on the necks of their camels.

The men of Israel said to Gideon, "Rule, my lord, over us. Both you, and your son, and your son's son, for you have saved us out of the hand of Midian."

Gideon said to them, "I will not rule, and my son will not rule over you. The Lord will rule over you."

Gideon said to them, "I will make a request of you, that you each give me an earring out of your plunder, as they had golden earrings because they were Ishmaelites."

They said, "We will certainly give them," and he opened his garment, and each man tossed into it an earring from his plunder. The weight of the golden earrings which he asked, was a thousand and seven hundred pieces of gold, besides the crescents, and the chains, and the garments, and the purple cloths that were on the kings of Midian, and besides the chains that were on the necks of their camels. Gideon made a vest from it and set it in his city in Ephrath.

All Israel went whoring after it there, and it became a stumbling block to Gideon and his house. Midian, was straightened before the Israelites, and they did not lift their head anymore, and the land had rest forty years in the days of Gideon. Jerubbaal the son of Joash went and sat in his house. Gideon had seventy sons begotten of his body, for he had many wives. His concubine in Shechem carried him a son and gave him the name Abimelech.

Gideon son of Joash died in his city, and he was buried in the sepulcher of Joash his father in Ephrath of Abi-Esdri. It happened when Gideon was dead, that the Israelites turned, and went whoring after Ba'als, and made for themselves a covenant with Ba'al that he should be their god. The Israelites did not remember the Lord God who had delivered them out of the hand of all that attacked them. They did not deal mercifully with the house of Jerubbaal (this is Gideon), according to all the good which he did for Israel.

Judges: Chapter 8 Notes

1 Codex Vaticanus: allophylôn (ⲀⲖⲖⲟⲫ︦ⲨⲖⲱⲚ).
Translation: foreigners (or aliens, gentiles)

- Codex Alexandrinus: huiôn anatolôn (ⲨⲓⲱⲚ
ⲀⲚⲀⲦⲞⲖⲱⲚ). Translation: sons of the easterners

- Aleppo Codex: bny qdm (בני קדם). Translation: sons of the
east (or easterners)

- Leningrad Codex: venei-kedem (בְנֵי־קֶדֶם). Translation:
sons of the east (or easterners)

- Targum Jerusalem: benei madincha (בְּנֵי מַדִנְחָא).
Translation: sons of east (or Medina)

As the sons of the east in this story are the Neshites, that
name is used in the translation.

2 Codex Vaticanus: parataxeôs Ares (ⲠⲀⲢⲀⲦⲀⲍⲈⲱⲤ
ⲀⲢⲈⲤ). Translation: phalanx (or side by side) of Ares

- Codex Alexandrinus: anabaseôs Ares (ⲀⲚⲀⲂⲀⲤⲈⲱⲤ
ⲀⲢⲈⲤ). Translation: ascent of Ares

- Aleppo Codex: mlmôlh hḥrs (מלמעלה החרס). Translation:
from above the destruction (or demolished, destroyed)

- Leningrad Codex: milma'aleh heChares (מִלְמַעֲלֵה הֶחָרֶס).
Translation: from above the Chares

- Targum Jerusalem: me'al shimsha (מֵעַל שִׁמְשָׁא).
Translation: upper (or fraudulent) sun (or servant, minister)

The Greeks transliterated Hrs as Ares, however, the Semitic term meant variations of 'destruction.' The Hebrew and Aramaic term also referred to pottery, clay, or ceramic, as did the cuneiform word ḫarši (𒄯) used in Nesite. In this case, the Greek translations and Masoretic interpretation seem consistent, as each of them interpreted the term as a proper name, suggesting a town named Heres, or if the Codex Alexandrinus is correct: Ascent of Heres. It is possible that Heres was the name of a god of destruction worshiped in Canaan, in which case it may have been the origin of the Greek Ares, whose origin is unclear.

As the sources do not agree on the word before Ares/Heres, the term 'Ascent of' is used from the Codex Alexandrinus, as that does seem consistent with the naming conventions of Canaanite towns.

3 Codex Vaticanus: ôs su ôs autoi eis omoiôma uiou basileôs (ⲱⲥ ⲥⲨ ⲱⲥ ⲀⲨⲦⲞⲒ ⲈⲒⲤ ⲞⲘⲞⲒⲰⲘⲀ ⲨⲒⲞⲨ ⲂⲀⲤⲒⲗⲈⲱⲤ). Translation: like you like himself (or he, she, it) into effigy son (or child) king (or chief, master lord)

• Codex Alexandrinus: ôsi sy omoeos soe, omoeos autôn, ôs idos morphê uiôn basileôn (ⲱⲥⲈⲒ ⲥⲨ ⲞⲘⲞⲒⲞⲤ ⲤⲞⲒ ⲞⲘⲞⲒⲞⲤ ⲀⲨⲦⲰⲚ ⲱⲥ ⲈⲒⲆⲞⲤ ⲘⲞⲣⳘⲏ ⲨⲒⲰⲚ ⲂⲀⲤⲒⲗⲈⲰⲚ). Translation: just as you resembling (or equal to) you resembling (or equal to) himself (or he, she, it), like the appearance (or kind, species, image) form (or appearance, kind, type) son (or child) king (or chief, master lord)

- Aleppo Codex: kmwk kmwhm åḥd ktår bny hmlk (כמון כמוהם אחד כתאר בני המלך). Translation: as like one of like the title (or rank, appearance) of the sons (or children, boys) of the king

- Leningrad Codex: kamovcha chemovhem echad keto'ar benei hammelech (כְּמוֹךָ כְּמוֹהֶם אֶחָד כְּתֹאַר בְּנֵי הַמֶּלֶךְ). Translation: as like one of like the title (or rank, appearance) of the sons (or children, boys) of the king

- Targum Jerusalem: me'al shimsha (מֵעַל שִׁמְשָׁא). Translation: upper (or fraudulent) sun (or servant, minister)

Judges: Chapter 9

Abimelech the son of Jerubbaal went to Shechem to his mother's brothers, and he said to them and all the families of the house of his mother's father, "Speak, I beg you, in the ears of all the men of Shechem, and say, 'Which is better for you? That seventy men, even all the sons of Jerubbaal, should reign over you, or that one man should reign over you? And remember that I am your bone and your flesh."

His mother's brothers spoke about him to all the men of Shechem, and their hearts turned towards Abimelech, and they said, "He is our brother. They gave him seventy pieces of silver out of the Temple of the Lord of the Covenant,[1] and Abimelech hired vain and cowardly men, and they followed him. He went to the house of his father in Ephrath and executed his brothers, the sons of Jerubbaal, seventy men on one stone. Jotham the youngest son of Jerubbaal was not executed, as he hid. All the men of Shechem and all the House of Millo were gathered together, and they made Abimelech king by the Oak of Sedition, which was at Shechem.

It was reported to Jotham, and he went and stood on the top of Mount Gerizim, and shouted to them, "Hear me, you men of Shechem, and God will hear you. The trees went out once on a time to anoint a king over them, and they said to the olive, 'Reign over us.' But the olive replied to them, 'Will I leave my fatness, with which men will glorify God, and go to be promoted over the trees?' The trees said to the fig tree, 'Come, reign over us.' But the fig tree replied to them, 'Will I leave my sweetness and my good fruits, and go to be promoted over the trees?' The trees said to the vine, 'Come, reign over us.' The vine replied to them, 'Will I leave my wine that gladdens God and men, and go to be promoted over the trees?' Then all the trees said to the bramble, 'Come, and reign over us.' The bramble replied to the trees, 'If you in truth anoint me to reign over you, come, stand under my shadow, and if not, let fire come out from me and devour the cedars of Lebanon.'"

"Now, if you have done it in truth and integrity, and have made Abimelech king. If you have worked well with Jerubbaal, and with his house. If you have done to him according to the reward of his hand, as my father fought for you, and put his life in jeopardy, and delivered you out of the hand of Midian, and you are risen up this day against the house of my father, and have slain his sons, being seventy men, on one stone, and have made Abimelech the son of his slave-woman king over the men of Shechem, because he is your brother. If then you have done truly and faithfully with Jerubbaal, and with his house today, rejoice in Abimelech, and let him also rejoice over you. But, if not, let fire come out from

Abimelech, and devour the men of Shechem, and the House of Millo, and let fire come out from the men of Shechem and the House of Millo, and devour Abimelech."

Jotham fled, and ran away and went as far as Beer, and lived there, out of the way of his brother Abimelech. Abimelech reigned over Israel for three years. God sent an evil spirit between Abimelech and the men of Shechem, and the men of Shechem dealt treacherously with the house of Abimelech, to bring the injury done to the seventy sons of Jerubbaal, and to lay their blood on their brother Abimelech, who killed them, and on the men of Shechem because they strengthened his hands to kill his brothers. The men of Shechem set men to lay in wait against him on the top of the mountains and robbed everyone who passed by them on the way, and it was reported to King Abimelech. Gaal the son of Jabal came, and his brothers, and passed by Shechem, and the men of Shechem trusted in him. They went out into the field, and gathered their grapes, and crushed them, and had a part, and they brought the grapes into the house of their god, and ate and drank, and cursed Abimelech.

Gaal the son of Jabal asked, "Who is Abimelech, and who is the son of Shechem, that we should serve him? Is he not the son of Jerubbaal, and is not Zebul his steward, his servant with the son of Hamor the father of

Shechem? Why should we serve him? If only these people were under my hand! I would then remove Abimelech, and I would say to him, 'Multiply your army, and come out.'"

Zebul the ruler of the city heard the words of Gaal the son of Jabal, and he was very angry. He sent messengers to Abimelech secretly, saying, "Look, Gaal the son of Jabal and his brothers have come to Shechem, and they have besieged the city against you. Now rise by night, you and the people with you, and lay wait in the field. It will come to pass in the morning at sunrise, you will rise early and approach the city, and he and the people with him will come out against you, and you will do to him according to your power."

Abimelech and all the people with him rose up by night and formed an ambuscade against Shechem in four companies. Gaal the son of Jabal went out and stood by the door of the gate of the city, and Abimelech and the people with him rose up from the ambuscade. Gaal the son of Jabal saw the people, and said to Zebul, "Look, people come down from the top of the mountain."

Zebul replied to him, "You see the shadow of the mountain as men."

Gaal continued and said, "Look, people come down from the west, from the area bordering the middle of the land, and another company comes by the road to the Oak of Visions."[2]

Zebul asked him, "Where is your mouth as you said, 'Who is Abimelech that we should serve him?' Are not these the people you despised? Go out now, and set the battle formation against him."

Gaal went out before the men of Shechem and set the battle formation against Abimelech. Abimelech pursued him, and he fled from before him, and many fell slain as far as the door of the gate. Abimelech entered into Arumah, and Zebul drove out Gaal and his brothers so that they should not live in Shechem. On the second day, people went out into their field, and one brought word to Abimelech. He took the people, and divided them into three companies, and formed an ambush in the field, and he looked, and the people went out of the city, and he rose up against them and struck them.

Abimelech and the chiefs of companies that were with him rushed forward and stood by the door of the gate of the city, and the two other companies rushed forward on all that were in the field and slaughtered them. Abimelech fought against the city all that day, and captured the city, and killed the people that were in it, and destroyed the city, and sowed it with salt.

All the men of the tower of Shechem heard and came to the gathering at the fortified Temple of the Lord of the Covenant.[3] It was reported to Abimelech, that all the men of the tower of Shechem were gathered together. Abimelech went up to Mount Zalmon, and all the people that were with him, and Abimelech took an ax in his hand, and cut down a branch of a tree, and took it, and laid it on his shoulders. He said to the people that were with him, "Follow my example, quickly,"

They cut down branches, each man, and followed Abimelech, and laid them against the place of gathering, and burnt the place of gathering with fire, and they died, all the men of the tower of Shechem, about a thousand men and women. Abimelech went out of the fortified temple of the covenant, and camped in Tubas[4] and captured it. There was a fortified tower in the middle of the city, where all the men and the women of the city fled and shut the door and went up on the roof of the tower. Abimelech approached the tower and besieged it.

When Abimelech approached the door of the tower to burn it with fire, a woman threw a piece of a millstone on his head and broke his skull. He cried out quickly to the young man, his armor-bearer, saying, "Draw your sword and kill me, so they should never say, 'A woman killed him,'" and the young man stabbed him through, and he died. The men of Israel saw that Abimelech was dead, and they went each to his place. So God repaid the wickedness of Abimelech, which he worked against his father, in slaying his seventy brothers. All the wickedness of the men of Shechem, God repaid on their head and also the curse of Jotham, the son of Jerubbaal.

Judges: Chapter 9 Notes

1 Codex Vaticanus: oecou Baalberith (ΟΙΚΟΥΒΑΑΛΒΕΡΙΘ). Translation: house of Ba'al-Berith

- Codex Alexandrinus: oecou Ba'al diathêcês (ΟΙΚΟΥΒΑΑΛ ΔΙΑΘΗΚΗϹ). Translation: house of Ba'al of the testament

- Aleppo Codex: byt bôl bryt (בית בעל ברית). Translation: Temple of the Lord of the Covenant

- Leningrad Codex: beit ba'al berit (בֵּית בַּעַל בְּרִית). Translation: Temple of the Lord of the Covenant

- Targum Jerusalem: beit ba'eil keyam (בֵּית בָּעֵיל קְיָם). Translation: Temple of the Lord of establishment

As Ba'al translates as 'Lord,' and berith translates as 'covenant' or 'testament,' the translation 'Temple of the Lord of the Covenant' is used.

2 Codex Vaticanus: êlônmaônenim (ΗΛΩΝΜΑΩΝΕΝΙΜ)

- Codex Alexandrinus: dryos apoblepontôn (ΔΡΥΟϹ ΑΠΟΒΛΕΠΟΝΤΩΝ). Translation: oak of visions

- Aleppo Codex: âlwn môwnnym (אלון מעוננים). Translation: oak of clouds (or diviners)

- Leningrad Codex: elovn me'ovnnim (אֵלוֹן מְעוֹנְנִים). Translation: oak of clouds (or diviners)

- Targum Jerusalem: meishar me'onenaya (מֵישַׁר מְעוֹנְנַיָּא). Translation: straight from Onnaya

The Greeks transliterated the words for 'oak of diviners' as ηλωνμαωνενιμ at the Library of Alexander, and later translated is as δρυος αποβλεποντων in the early Christian Era. While the term was a proper name, the name also had a meaning, and therefore this translation uses the later translation found in the Codex Alexandrinus. It is possible that this oak was one of the Asherah trees that were later banned by King Josiah in circa 625 BC.

3 Codex Vaticanus: syneleusin Baethêlberith (ϹΥΝΕΛΕΥϹΙΝ ΒΑΙΘΗΛΒΕΡΙΘ). Translation: meeting place (or coming together) Baethêlberith

• Codex Alexandrinus: to ochyrôma oecou tou Ba'al diathêcês (ΤΟ ΟΧΥΡѠΜΑ ΟΙΚΟΥ ΤΟΥ ΒΑΑΛ ΔΙΑΘΗΚΗϹ). Translation: the fortified house (or temple) the Ba'al covenant

• Aleppo Codex: sryh byt ål bryt (צְרִיח בֵּית אֵל בְּרִית). Translation: fortified house (or temple) god covenant

• Leningrad Codex: tzeriach veit El berit (צְרִיחַ בֵּית אֵל בְּרִית). Translation: fortified temple god covenant

• Targum Jerusalem: veit El lemigzar keyam (בֵּית אֵל לְמִגְזַר קְיָם). Translation: temple god of the separation of establishment

The Codex Vaticanus and Masoretic Text are phonetically similar here, however, the 5th century AD Codex Alexandrinus has a significant deviation. The earlier Greek translation from the Library of Alexandria appears to have transliterated the term preserved in the Masoretic Text as byt âl bryt (בית אל ברית) as Baethêlberith (Βαιθηλβεριθ), indicating it was viewed as a proper name. The later Codex Alexandrinus translation, from the 5th century AD, which was based on the Hebrew translation in circulation at the time, refers to the Ba'al of the Covenant instead of the god of the Covenant. As the Greeks could not have transliterated a word that was not in the Hebrew text, the term must have been present at the time, however, the earlier Vaticanus Codex supports the text found in the Masoretic Text as having also been in the Aramaic version of Judges that the Greeks translated in the 3rd century BC.

It isn't clear where the version of the verse preserved in the Codex Alexandrinus came from, however, must have been Aramaic, suggesting the verse was edited to change the 'Temple of the God of the Covenant' to a temple of some ba'al. As this temple was in Shechem, it was likely part of the Hasmonean anti-Samaritan propaganda between 113 and 69 BC. The fact that the Temple of the God of the Covenant already existed in Shechem before the time of Solomon supports the Samaritan claim that Solomon's Temple was not the original temple of their God, as Shechem was the ancient capital of Samaria.

4 Codex Vaticanus: Thêbês (ΘΗΒΗC)

- Codex Alexandrinus: Thebes (ΘΕΒΕC)

- Aleppo Codex: Tbṣ (תבץ)

- Leningrad Codex: Tevetz (תֵּבֵץ)

- Targum Jerusalem: Tevetz (תֵבֵץ)

This is believed by some to be a reference to the city of Tubas (طوباس) in the northern area of the modern Palestinian West Bank, which is near Mount Gerizim, and so the name Tubas is used in this translation.

Judges: Chapter 10

After Abimelech, Tola the son of Puah rose up to save Israel, being the son of his father's brother, an Issacharite, and he lived in Samaria[1] in the mountains of Ephraim. He judged Israel twenty-three years, and died, and was buried in Samaria. After him arose Jair of Gilead, and he judged Israel twenty-two years. He had thirty-two sons riding on thirty-two colts, and they had thirty-two cities, and they called them Jair's towns until this day in the land of Gilead. Jair died and was buried in Ramnon.[2] The Israelites did evil again in the sight of the Lord and served the Lords and Ashteroths, the gods of Arameans, Sidonians, Moabites, Ammonites, and Pelesets, and they forgot the Lord and did not serve him. The Lord was very angry with Israel and sold them into the hands of the Pelesets and the hands of the Ammonites. They afflicted and bruised all the Israelites beyond Jordan in the land of the Amorites in Gilead at that time and for eighteen years. The Ammonites crossed the Jordan to attack Judah, Benjamin, and Ephraim, and the Israelites were greatly afflicted. The Israelites cried to the Lord, "We have sinned against you because we have forgotten God and served the Lords."

The Lord said to the Israelites, "Didn't I save you from Egypt and the Amorites, and from the sons of Ammon (and Moab),[3] and from the Pelesets, and from the Sidonians, Amalekites, and Midianites[4] who afflicted you?

And you cried to me, and I saved you out of their hands? Yet you forgot me and served other gods, therefore I will not save you anymore. Go, and pray to the gods who you have chosen for yourselves, and let them save you in the time of your affliction."

The Israelites said to the Lord, "We have sinned. Do to us whatever is good in your eyes, but save us this day."

They put away the foreign gods from among them and served only the Lord, and his mind was pained for the trouble of Israel. The Ammonites went up and camped in Gilead, and the Israelites were gathered together and camped on the hill. The people and the princes of Gilead said each man to his neighbor, "Who is he that will begin to fight against the Ammonites? He will be the head over all that live in Gilead."

Judges: Chapter 10 Notes

1 Codex Vaticanus: Samir (ϲΑΜιΡ)

- Codex Alexandrinus: Samaria (ϲΑΜΑΡΕιΑ)

- Aleppo Codex: Šmyr (שָׁמִיר). Translation: dill, emery-stone, brier, flint, thistle, adamant, fennel, batch, aggregate, bribe

  - Leningrad Codex: Shamir (שָׁמִיר). Translation: dill, emery-stone, brier, flint, thistle, adamant, fennel, batch, aggregate, bribe

  - Targum Jerusalem: Shamir (שָׁמִי). Translation: dill, emery-stone, brier, flint, thistle, adamant, fennel, batch, aggregate, bribe

Lucian's version of the Septuagint deviates from both the Codex Vaticanus and Masoretic Text at this point, however, it is not clear if he had a Hebrew or Aramaic copy of Judges which included the word Samaria (שומרון), or simply interpreted Šmyr (שמיר) as Samaria. The term may be a relic of the Akkadian version of Judges, as the land was known as ᵏᵘʳSamerina (𒆳𒊠𒈨𒊑𒈾) in Cuneiform, meaning 'land Samerina.' In any event, Shamir does appear to be a reference to the land that would later be called Samaria, and therefore the Codex Alexandrinus is followed.

2 Codex Vaticanus: Ramnôn (ΡΑΜΝωΝ)

- Codex Alexandrinus: Rammô (ΡΑΜΜω)

- Aleppo Codex: Qmwn (קָמוֹן)

- Leningrad Codex: Kamovn (קָמוֹן)

- Targum Jerusalem: Kamovn (קָמוֹן)

This location is unknown today, however, would have been in northwest Jordan. As both versions of the Septuagint generally agree, the Greek name is retained.

3 Codex Vaticanus: cai apo uiôn Ammôn (ΚΑΙΑΠΟΥΙϢΝ ΑΜΜϢΝ). Translation: and from sons of Ammon

- Codex Alexandrinus: cae oe uioe Ammôn cae Môab (ΚΑΙ ΟΙΥΙΟΙΑΜΜϢΝΚΑΙΜϢΑΒ). Translation: and of the sons of Ammon and Moab

- Aleppo Codex: wmn bny Ômwn (ומן בני עמון). Translation: and from the sons of Ammon

- Leningrad Codex: umin-benei Ammovn (וּמִן־בְּנֵי עַמּוֹן). Translation: and from the sons of Ammon

- Targum Jerusalem: umin emora'ah umin benei Amon (וּמִן אֱמוֹרָאָה וּמִן בְּנֵי עַמּוֹן). Translation: and from the speakers and the sons of Ammon

As Moab is only mentioned in the Codex Alexandrinus, is may be a later scribal note, and is therefore placed in parentheses. It is unclear if it was the source of the Targum Jerusalem's 'speakers' as the words are similar. It is possible that the term Moabite was mistranslated from the term 'speaker' in the targums of the era.

4 Codex Vaticanus: Sidôniôn cae Amalêc cae Madiam
(ϹΙΔѠΝΙѠΝ ΚΑΙ ΑΜΑΛΗΚ ΚΑΙ ΜΑΔΙΑΜ). Translation:
Sidonians and Amalakites and Midianites

• Codex Alexandrinus: Sidônioe cae Madiam cae Amalêc
(ϹΙΔѠΝΙΟΙ ΚΑΙ ΜΑΔΙΑΜ ΚΑΙ ΑΜΑΛΗΚ). Translation:
Sidonians and Madianites and Amakites

• Aleppo Codex: sydwnym wômlq wmôwn (צידונים ועמלק
ומעון). Translation: Sidonians and Amalakite and abode (or
dwelling)

• Leningrad Codex: Tzidovnim va'Amalek uma'ovn
(צִידוֹנִים וַעֲמָלֵק וּמָעוֹן). Translation: Sidonians and Amalakites
and abode (or dwelling)

• Targum Jerusalem: Tzidona'ei va'Amalka'ei ve'enashei
(צִידוֹנָאֵי וַעֲמָלְקָאֵי וֶאֱנָשֵׁי). Translation: Sidonians and Amalakites
and people

The Hebrew term ma'ovn (מָעוֹן) in the Masoretic Text is
not the same as the name Midian (Μαδιαμ) in the Septuagint,
however, is likely a transcription error from Midyan (מִדְיָן),
as it only appears once in Masoretic Judges.

Judges: Chapter 11

Jephthah the Gileadite was a mighty man, but he was the son of a prostitute who carried Jephthah for Gilead. The wife of Gilead carried his sons, and the sons of his wife grew up, and they drove out Jephthah, and said to him, "You will not inherit from the house of our father as you are the son of a concubine!"

Jephthah fled from the face of his brothers and lived in the land of Tob, and vain men gathered around Jephthah and went out with him. It happened when the Ammonites prepared to fight with Israel, that the elders of Gilead went to fetch Jephthah from the land of Tob.[1]

They said to Jephthah, "Come, and be our leader, and we will fight with the Ammonites."

Jephthah said to the elders of Gilead, "Did you not hate me, and drive me out of my father's house, and banish me from you? And now you have come to me when you need me?"

The elders of Gilead said to Jephthah, "We have now turned to you that you should go with us and fight against the Ammonites, and be our head over all the inhabitants of Gilead."

Jephthah said to the elders of Gilead, "If you turn back to me to fight with the Ammonites and the Lord should deliver them before me then will I be your leader."

The elders of Gilead said to Jephthah, "The Lord be a witness between us if we do not do according to your word."

Jephthah went with the elders of Gilead, and the people made him head and ruler over them, and Jephthah spoke before the Lord in Mizpeh. Jephthah sent messengers to the king of Ammon, saying, "What have I to do with you, that you have come against me to fight in my land?"

The king of Ammon said to the messengers of Jephthah, "Israel took my land when he went up out of Egypt, from Arnon to Jabbok, and to the Jordan, now then, return it peaceably and I will leave."

Jephthah again sent messengers to the king of Ammon, who said to him, "Jephthah says, 'Israel did not take the land of Moab, or the land of Ammon, in their going up out of Egypt, Israel went in the wilderness as far as the Papyrus Sea[2] and came to Kadesh. Israel also sent to the king of Moab, and he did not consent, and Israel stayed in Kadesh. They journeyed in the wilderness and circumnavigated the land of Edom and the land of Moab. They traveled to the east of the land of Moab, and camped in the country beyond Arnon, and did not enter into the borders of Moab, as Arnon is the border of Moab. Israel sent messengers to Sihon king of the Amorites and the king of Heshbon, and Israel said to him, 'Let us pass, we beg you, through your land to our place.' Sihon did not trust Israel to pass by his borders, and Sihon gathered all his people, and they camped at Jahaz, and he set the battle formation against Israel."

"Lord the god of Israel delivered Sihon and all his people into the hand of Israel, and they slaughtered him, and Israel inherited all the land of the Amorites who lived in that land, from Arnon and to Jabbok, and from the wilderness to the Jordan. Now Lord the god of Israel has removed the Amorites from before his people Israel, and will you inherit his land? Won't you inherit the possessions which Chemosh your god will cause you to inherit? Won't we inherit the land of all those who Lord the god has removed from before you? Now, are you any better than Balak son of Zippor, king of Moab? Did he not fight with Israel and make war with them when Israel lived in Heshbon and in its borders, and in the land of Aroer and in its borders, and in all the cities by the Jordan for three hundred years? And did you recover them at that time? Now I have not sinned against you, but you wrong me in preparing war against me. Now decide, Lord Judge,[3] today between the Israelites and the Ammonites."

But the king of Ammon did not listen to the words of Jephthah, which he sent to him. The spirit of the Lord came on Jephthah and he passed through Gilead and Manasseh and passed by the watch-tower of Gilead to the other side of the Ammonites. Jephthah vowed a vow to the Lord, saying, "If you will indeed deliver the Ammonites into my hand, then it will come to pass that whoever will first come out of the door of my house to meet me when I return in peace from the Ammonites, he will be the Lord's, and I will offer him up for a whole burnt offering."

Jephthah advanced to meet the Ammonites to fight against them, and the Lord delivered them into his hand. He slaughtered them from Aroer all the way to Arnon,[4] in twenty cities, and as far as Abel's vineyard[5] with massive great destruction. The Ammonites were straightened before the Israelites, and Jephthah returned to his house in Mizpeh and saw his daughter come out to meet him dancing with tambourines. She was his only child, he had no other son or daughter. When he saw her, he tore his clothes, and said, "Oh, oh, my daughter! You have indeed troubled me, and you are the cause of my trouble! I have vowed against you to the Lord, and I will not be able to return from it!"

She said to him, "Father, have you vowed to the Lord? Do to me accordingly as the words of your mouth, in that the Lord has worked vengeance for you on your enemies of the Ammonites. Let my father now do this thing. Leave me alone for two months, and I will go up and down in the mountains, and I will mourn my virginity with my friends."

He said, "Go," and he sent her away for two months. She went with her friends, and mourned her virginity in the mountains. It happened at the end of the two months that she returned to her father, and he performed her his vow which he vowed, and she had known no man. It was an ordinance in Israel, that the daughters of Israel went from year to year to mourn the daughter of Jephthah the Gileadite for four days in a year.

Judges: Chapter 11 Notes

1 Codex Vaticanus: Tôb (ΤⲱB)

- Aleppo Codex: Twb (טוב)

- Leningrad Codex: Tovv (טֽוֹב)

- Targum Jerusalem: tava (טָבָא). Translation: rumor

The town of Tob is believed to have been in Amman southeast of the Sea of Galilee. It is generally accepted that it is the town of Tubu (𒌅𒁕) mentioned in the Amarna Letter EA205 from circa 1350 BC.

2 Codex Vaticanus: thalassês Siph (ⲐⲀⲗⲀⲤⲤⲎⲤⲤⲓⲫ). Translation: Siph Sea

- Codex Alexandrinus: thalassês erythras (ⲐⲀⲗⲀⲤⲤⲎⲤ ⲉⲢⲨⲐⲢⲀⲤ). Translation: Erythrean Sea

- Aleppo Codex: ym swp (ים סוף). Translation: Papyrus (or reed) Sea

- Leningrad Codex: yam-Suf (יַם־סֽוּף). Translation: Papyrus (or reed) Sea

- Targum Jerusalem: yama deSuf (יְמָא דְסוּף). Translation: sea of papyrus (or reeds)

The older Codex Vaticanus maintains the Greek transliteration of the name the Suf (סֽוּף) Sea as Siph (Σιφ) Sea, while the later Codex Alexandrinus uses the more common Greek translation of Erythrean ('Ερυθρᾶσ) Sea. The confirms that the Aramaic text the Greeks translated included the name Swf Sea. Both the Aramaic swf (סוּף) and Phoenician term swf (סוּף), meaning papyrus plants, were adopted from the Egyptian term tjufi (𓈖𓏏𓆰𓏤), which referred to papyrus, papyrus plants, and papyrus marshes. The Egyptian term continued to be used into the Classical era as the Coptic words čoouf (ϫⲟⲟⲩϥ), conf (ϭⲟⲛϥ), and comf (ϭⲟⲙϥ), all meaning papyrus. Conversely, the Egyptian name of the Red Sea was the Sea of Heh (𓎛), meaning 'very large sea' from the Middle Kingdom era onward, however, it is believed to have originally been named after the ancient Egyptian frog god Heh (𓎛𓎛). As the Greek translation of Erythrean Sea is anachronistic, the translation of Papyrus Sea is imported from the Masoretic Text.

3 Codex Vaticanus: crinae c̄s̄ crinôn (ΚΡΙΝΑΙΚϹΚΡΙΝΩΝ). Translation: decide Lord Judge

• Codex Alexandrinus: crinae cyrios o crinôn (ΚΡΙΝΑΙ ΚΥΡΙΟϹΟΚΡΙΝΩΝ). Translation: decide lord the judge

• Aleppo Codex: yšpt Yhwh hšpt (ישפט יהוה השפט). Translation: will decide Yhwh the judge

• Leningrad Codex: yishpot Yehvah hashofet (יִשְׁפֹּט יְהוָה הַשֹּׁפֵט). Translation: will decide Yehvah the judge

• Targum Jerusalem: yedin Yeyah da'avad dina (יְדִין יְיָ דַּעֲבַד דִינָא). Translation: powers of Yahw the slave (or servant) of law (or judgment)

As Shofet does not appear to be the name of a Canaanite god, in the Septuagint's version of Judges Jephthah is recognizing the King of Amman as a Lord Judge, implying the King of Amman is one of Egypt's local magistrates under Ramesses II and Merneptah. As Amman was one of the few Canaanite cities not listed as being in revolt during the reign of Merneptah, while Israel was listed as being in revolt, it seems this story of Jephthah's revolt against Amman was the Israelite revolt listed in Egyptian records.

4 Codex Vaticanus: Arnôn (ΑΡΝШΝ).

- Codex Alexandrinus: Semôith (ϹΕΜШΙϴ)

- Aleppo Codex: Mnyt (מנית)

- Leningrad Codex: Minnit (מִנִּית)

- Targum Jerusalem: Minit (מְנִית)

As none of the sources agree, the oldest source-text, the Codex Vaticanus' Arnon is used in this translation. The Arnon stream is generally accepted as being the Wadi Mujib river canyon in Jordan, approximately 90 km (56 miles) south of Amman.

5 Codex Vaticanus: Ebelcharmin (ΕΒΕΛΧΑΡΜΙΝ).

- Codex Alexandrinus: Abel ampelônô (ΑΒΕΛ ΑΜΠΕΛШΝШ). Translation: Abel's vineyard

- Aleppo Codex: Åbl krmym (**אבל כרמים**). Translation: Abel's vineyard

- Leningrad Codex: Avel keramim (אָבֵל כְּרָמִים). Translation: Abel's vineyard

- Targum Jerusalem: yshar keramaya (יְשַׁר כְּרְמַיָא). Translation: directly to (or even) vineyard

As the Codex Vaticanus includes a transliteration of the name found in the Masoretic Text, and the Codex Alexandrinus includes a translation of the name found in the Masoretic Text, the Masoretic name is imported.

Judges: Chapter 12

The Ephraimites assembled and went to the north, and said to Jephthah, "Why did you go and fight Amman, and did not call us to go with you? We will burn your house!"

Jephthah answered them, "I and my people and Amman were engaged in war, and I called for you, and you did not save me out of their hand. I saw that you were no ally, and I took my life in my own hand and invaded Amman, and the Lord delivered them into my hand. Why have you come up against me today to fight with me?" Jephthah gathered all the men of Gilead and fought with Ephraim, and the men of Gilead slaughtered Ephraim, because they that escaped of Ephraim said, "You are of Gilead among Ephraim and among Manasseh."

Gilead took the fords of the Jordan near Ephraim, and they who escaped among the Ephraimites said to them, "Let us go across," and the men of Gilead asked, "Are you an Ephraimite?"

He answered, "No."

Then they said to him, "Now say, 'stalk of grain,'"[1] and he did not pronounce it right, so they captured him and killed him at the fords of the Jordan. Forty-two thousand Ephraimites died there at that time. Jephthah judged Israel six years, and Jephthah the Gileadite died and was buried in his city in Gilead.

After him, Ibzan of the Temple of Lehem[2] judged Israel. He had thirty sons, and thirty daughters, who he sent out, and he brought in thirty daughters for his sons from outside, and he judged Israel seven years. Ibzan died and was buried at the Temple of Lehem. After him, Elon of Zebulun judged Israel for ten years. Elon of Zebulun died and was buried in Aijalon in the land of Zebulun.

After him, Abdon the son of Hillel, a Per-Atenite, judged Israel. He had forty sons, and thirty grandsons, that rode on seventy colts, and he judged Israel eight years. Abdon the son of Hillel, the Per-Atenite, died and was buried in Per-Aten[3] in the land of Ephraim in the mountains of Amalek.

Judges: Chapter 12 Notes

1 Codex Vaticanus: stachys (ϲⲧⲁⲭⲩϲ). Translation: stalk of grain (or progeny)

• Codex Alexandrinus: synthêma (ϲⲩⲛⲑⲏⲙⲁ). Translation: anything agreed upon

• Aleppo Codex: šblt (שבלת). Translation: stalk of grain

• Leningrad Codex: shibbolet (שִׁבֹּלֶת). Translation: stalk of grain

• Targum Jerusalem: shubbalta (שׁוּבַּלְתָּא). Translation: stalk of grain (or branch of river)

The spelling of šblt (שבלת) in the Masoretic Text is not the Hebrew spelling of šybwlt (שיבולת), but the older Canaanite spelling, recorded as šblt (𐎌𐎁𐎍) in Ugaritic Canaanite, and šblt (𐤔𐤁𐤋𐤕) in Phoenician Canaanite. This older Canaanite spelling developed into the Hebrew spelling during the Persian era, under the influence of Imperial Aramaic. The Aramaic spelling found in the Targum Jerusalem is virtually identical to the older Akkadian cuneiform term šubulta (𒈗𒌓𒁀𒌈), indicating that the division among the Israelites was already between those speaking Canaanite versus Aramaic. Arameans appeared in Mesopotamian records centuries earlier than the Habirus, and the two cultures were generally described as inhabiting the same regions, although the Arameans were more urban, and the Habirus were more nomadic.

2 Codex Vaticanus: Baethleem (ΒΑΙΘΛΕΕΜ)

- Aleppo Codex: byt lhm (בית לחם). Translation: house (or temple) of Lehem (or grain)

- Leningrad Codex: beit Lachem (בֵּית לָחֶם). Translation: house (or temple) of Lehem (or grain)

- Targum Jerusalem: beit Lechem (בֵּית לֶחֶם). Translation: house (or temple) of Lehem (or grain)

Lehem was an ancient Canaanite god of grain, rebirth, and life, similar in nature to the Egyptian god Osiris, and Greek god Dionysus. Lehem was also the word meaning 'grain,' meaning the name could be interpreted as anything from the 'Temple of Lehem' to the 'grain silo,' however, the ancient Samaritan city of Bethlehem is being referenced, which was named after the Temple of Lehem, and so the name is translated directly from the Masoretic text.

3 Codex Vaticanus: Pharathôm (ΦΑΡΑΘΩΜ).

- Codex Alexandrinus: Phraathôn (ΦΡΑΑΘΩΝ)

- Aleppo Codex: prôtwn (פרעתון)

- Leningrad Codex: Fir'atovn (פִּרְעָתוֹן)

- Targum Jerusalem: Fir'atovn (פִּרְעָתוֹן)

The Hebrew name is a translation of an Egyptian name, Per-Aten. It is unknown where the town of Per-Aten (or Per-Atum) in the land of Ephraim was located, however, it seems evident that it started as an Egyptian colony during the New Kingdom era. As it was named Per-Aten (𓉐𓇋𓏏𓇳) the foundation of the colony would have almost certainly taken place during the Amarna Period, between 1353-1336 BC. During that era, Ephraim was ruled by the Judges Ehud and Shamgar, and the land was described as being at peace until the end of the era.

Judges: Chapter 13

The Israelites again committed iniquity before the Lord, and the Lord delivered them into the hands of the Pelesets for forty years. There was a man of Zorah, of the family of the Danites whose name was Manoah, and his wife was barren and did not become pregnant.

The messenger of the lord appeared to the woman, and said to her, "Look, you are barren and have not carried, yet you will conceive a son. Now be very cautious, and drink no wine or strong drink, and eat nothing unclean, as you are with child, and will give birth to a son. No iron must touch his head, for the child will be a Nazarite to God from the womb, and he will begin to save Israel from the hand of the Pelesets."

The woman went in, and told her husband, "A man of God came to me, and he looked like a messenger of God, very dreadful, and I did not ask him from where he was, and he did not tell me his name. He said to me, 'Look, you are with child and will give birth to a son, and now drink no wine or strong drink, and eat nothing unclean, for the child will be holy to God from the womb until the day of his death."

Manoah prayed to the Lord, "If you, Lord, sent to me a man of God, let him now come to us once more, and teach us what we will do to the child about to be born."

The Lord heard the voice of Manoah, and the messenger of God came again to the woman, as she sat in the field, and Manoah her husband was not with her. The woman rushed, and ran to bring word to her husband, and said to him, "Look the man who came to me the other day has appeared to me."

Manoah arose and followed his wife, and came to the man, and said to him, "Are you the man that spoke to the woman?"

The messenger answered, "I am."

Manoah said, "Now your word will come to pass. How will we judge the child and our dealings with him?"

The messenger of the lord said to Manoah, "Of all things concerning which I spoke to the woman, she will beware. She will eat nothing that comes of the vine yielding wine, and let her not drink wine or strong liquor, and let her not eat anything unclean. All the things that I have ordered her she will observe."

Manoah said to the messenger of the lord, "Let us keep you here, and prepare for you a kid of the goats."

The messenger of the lord replied to Manoah, "If you should detain me, I will not eat of your bread, and if you would offer a whole burnt offering, to the Lord you will offer it."

Manoah did not know that he was the messenger of the lord. Manoah said to the messenger of the lord, "What is your name, that when your word will come to pass, we may glorify you?"

The messenger of the lord said to him, "Why do you ask my name when it is wonderful?"

Manoah took a kid of the goats and its meat offering and offered it on the rock to the Lord, and the messenger worked a distinct work, and Manoah and his wife were looking on. It happened when the flame went up above the altar towards the sky, that the messenger of the lord went up in the flame, and Manoah and his wife were looking, and they fell on their face to the earth. The messenger did not appear again to Manoah or his wife. Then Manoah knew that this was the messenger of the lord. Manoah said to his wife, "We will certainly die because we have seen God."

But his wife said to him, "If the Lord wanted to kill us, he would not have received from our hand a whole burnt offering and a meat offering. He would not have shown us all these things, and he would have made us hear all these things."

The woman gave birth to a son, and she called his name Samson, and the child grew, and the Lord blessed him. The spirit of the Lord began to go out with him in the camp of Dan and between Zorah and Esthaol.

Judges: Chapter 14

Samson went down to Timnah and saw a woman in Timnah from the daughters of the Pelesets. He returned and told his father and his mother, and said, "I have seen a woman in Timnah of the daughters of the Pelesets, and now procure her for me as a wife."

His father and his mother replied to him, "Are there no daughters of your brothers, and is there not a woman of all my people, that you go to take a wife instead of from the uncircumcised Pelesets?"

Samson said to his father, "Take her for me, as she is good-looking."

His father and his mother did not know that it was of the Lord. That he wanted to take revenge on the Pelesets. At that time the Pelesets lorded over Israel. Samson and his father and mother went down to Timnah, and he came to the vineyard of Timnah. A young lion roared in meeting him. The spirit of the Lord came powerfully over him, and he crushed him as he would have killed a kid of the goats, barehanded. He did not tell his father and his mother what he had done.

They went down and spoke to the woman, and she was beautiful in the eyes of Samson. After some time he returned to take her, and he turned aside to see the carcass of the lion, and in the mouth of the lion was a hive of bees with honey. He collected some and ate some, and he took some to his father and mother and gave it to them, and they also ate, but he did not tell them that he took the honey out of the mouth of the lion. His father went down to the woman, and Samson made a banquet there for seven days, as the young men used to. When they saw him they took thirty guests and joined him.

Samson said to them, "I propound a riddle for you. If you will answer it for me, and solve it within the seven days of the feast, I will give you thirty sheets and thirty changes of clothing. If you can't answer it for me, you will give me thirty sheets and thirty changes of clothing."

They answered him, "Propound your riddle, and we will hear it."

He said to them, "Meat came out of the eater, and sweetness out of the strong."

They could not answer the riddle for three days. On the fourth day, they said to the wife of Samson, "Deceive now your husband and let him tell you the riddle, in case we burn you and your father's house with fire. Did you invite us to do violence?"

Samson's wife wept in front of him, and said, "You hate me, and don't love me! The riddle which you have propounded to my people, you have not told me."

Samson said to her, "If I have not told it to my father and my mother, will I tell it to you?"

She wept in front of him seven days, during which their banquet lasted, and on the seventh day, he told her because she troubled him, and she told it to her people. The men of the city said to him on the seventh day, before sunrise, "What is sweeter than honey, and what is stronger than a lion?"

Samson said to them, "If you had not plowed with my heifer, you would not have known my riddle."

The Spirit of the Lord came on him powerfully, and he went down to Ashkelon, and murdered thirty of the men that lived there, and took their clothes, and gave the changes of clothing to those that answered the riddle. Samson was very angry and went back to the house of his father. The wife of Samson was given to one of his friends that he was close with.

Judges: Chapter 15

In the days of wheat harvest, Samson visited his wife with a kid, and said, "I will go to my wife to the bedchamber, but her father did not allow him to go."

Her father said, "I said that you did certainly hate her, and I gave her to one of your friends. Is not her younger sister better than she? Let her be for you instead of her."

Samson said to them, "For once am I blameless among the Pelesets, even though I cause problems among them."

Samson went and caught three hundred foxes, and took torches, and turned tail to tail, and put a torch between two tails, and fastened it. He set fire to the torches and sent the foxes into the grain of the Pelesets, and everything was burnt from the threshing floor to the standing grain, including the vineyard and olives.

The Pelesets inquired, "Who has done these things?"

They answered, "Samson the son-in-law of the Timnahite, because he has taken his wife, and given her to one of his friends.

The Pelesets went up and burnt her and her father's house with fire. Samson said to them, "Though you may have dealt so with her, verily I will be avenged against you, and afterward I will stop."

He knocked them down, and ran down and hid in a cave of the rock Etam. The Pelesets went up, and camped in Judah, and spread themselves abroad in Lehi. The men of Judah asked, "Why have you come up against us?"

The Pelesets answered, "We have come up to catch Samson, and to do to him as he has done to us."

The three thousand men of Judah went down to the cave in the rock Etam, and they said to Samson, "Don't you know that the Pelesets rule over us? What is this that you have done to us?"

Samson answered to them, "As they did to me, so have I done to them."

They said to him, "We have come down to catch you and deliver you into the hand of the Pelesets."

Samson replied to them, "Swear to me that you will not kill me yourselves."

They answered him, "No, we will only tie you tight, and deliver you into their hand, and will not kill you," and they tied him with two new ropes, and brought him from that rock.

They came to Lehi, and the Pelesets shouted, and ran to meet him, and the Spirit of the Lord came mightily on him, and the ropes that were on his arms became as kindling which is burnt with fire, and his bonds were consumed from off his hands. He found the jaw-bone of a donkey that had been thrown away, and he took it in his hand and killed a thousand men with it.

Samson said, "With the jaw-bone of a donkey I have completely destroyed them, for with the jaw-bone of a donkey I have slaughtered a thousand men!"

When he stopped speaking, then he threw the jaw-bone from his hand, and he called that place Raising-the-Jaw-Bone. He was very thirsty, and wept before the Lord, and said, "You were willing to grant this great deliverance by the hand of your servant, but now I will die from thirst, and fall into the hand of the uncircumcised?" He was very thirsty, and wept before the Lord, and said, "You were willing to grant this great deliverance by the hand of your servant, but now will I die from thirst, and fall into the hand of the uncircumcised?"

God broke open a hollow place in the jaw, and there came out water, and he drank, and his spirit returned and he revived. Therefore the name of the fountain was called The Well of the Invoker, which is in Lehi until this day. He judged Israel in the days of the Pelesets twenty years.

Judges: Chapter 16

Samson went to Gaza, and visited a prostitute there, and went into her. It was reported to the Gazites, saying, "Samson has come here," and they surrounded him and laid wait for him all night at the gate of the city, and they were quiet all the night, saying, "Let's wait until the dawn, and we'll kill him."

Samson slept until midnight, and rose up at midnight, and took hold of the doors of the gate of the city with the two posts, and lifted them up with the bar, and laid them on his shoulders, and he went up to the top of the mountain that is before Hebron and laid them there. After this, he loved a woman in Sorek, and her name was Delilah. The princes of the Pelesets came up to her, and said to her, "Seduce him, and see where his great strength comes from, and how we will prevail against him, and bind him to humble him, and we will give you each eleven hundred pieces of silver."

Delilah said to Samson, "Tell me, I beg you, what is your great strength, and how will you be bound that you may be humbled?

Samson said to her, "If they tie me with seven moist cords that have not been stretched, then I will be as weak as one of the ordinary men."

The princes of the Pelesets brought her seven moist cords that had not been stretched, and she tied him with them. The men were hiding in her chamber, and she said to him, "The Pelesets are on you, Samson!"

He broke the cords like anyone would break a thread when it has touched the fire, and his strength was unknown. Delilah said to Samson, "Look, you have cheated me, and told me lies. Now then tell me how you will be tied."

He said to her, "If they should tie me fast with new ropes with which work has not been done, then will I be as weak as another man."

Delilah took new ropes and tied him with them, and the men that were hiding, came out of the chamber, and she said, "The Pelesets are on you, Samson,' and he broke them off his arms like a thread."

Delilah said to Samson, "Look, you have deceived me, and told me lies. Tell me, I demand of you, how you may be tied."

He said to her, "If you should braid the seven locks of my head with a braid, and should fasten them with the pin into the wall, then I will be weak as another man."

When he was asleep, Delilah took the seven locks of his head, and braided them into a braid, and fastened them with the pin into the wall, and she shouted, "The Pelesets are on you, Samson!"

He awoke out of his sleep and pulled the pin of the braid out of the wall. Delilah said to Samson, "How can you say, 'I love you,' when your heart is not with me? This third time you have deceived me, and have not told me where your great strength is."

She hurt him with her words and chastised him so much that his spirit failed almost to death. Then he told her all his heart, and said to her, "A razor has not come on my head, because I have been a holy one of God from my mother's womb. If then I should be shaven, my strength will leave from me, and I will be weak, and I will be like all other men."

Delilah saw that he told her all his heart, and she sent and called the princes of the Pelesets, saying, "Come up one more time, as he has told me all his heart."

The chiefs of the Pelesets went up to her and brought the money in their hands. Delilah made Samson sleep on her knees, and she called a man, and he shaved the seven locks of his head, and she began to humble him, and his strength departed from him. Delilah yelled, "The Pelesets are on you Samson!"

He woke out of his sleep and said, "I will go out as I did before, and shake myself," and he did not know that the Lord was departed from him. The Pelesets took him, and cut out his eyes, and brought him down to Gaza, and bound him with brass shackles, and he ground grain in the prison-house. The hair of his head began to grow as before it was shaven.

The chiefs of the Pelesets met to offer a great sacrifice to their god Dagon, and to celebrate, and they said, "God has given into our hand our enemy Samson." The people saw him, and sang praises to their god, "Our god," they said, "has delivered into our hand our enemy, who destroyed our land, and who murdered many of us."

When their heart was happy, they said, "Call Samson out of the prison-house, and let him play before us," and they called Samson out of the prison-house, and he played before them. They slapped him with the palms of their hands and tied him between the pillars.

Samson said to the young man that guided him, "Allow me to feel the pillars on which the house rests, so I can lean on them."

The house was full of men and women and all the chiefs of the Pelesets were there, and on the roof were about three thousand men and women looking at the sports of Samson. Samson wept before the Lord, and said, "Lord, my lord! Remember me, I beg you, and strengthen me, God, just this once, and I will repay the Pelesets for my eyes."

Samson took hold of the two pillars which supported the house, and leaned on them, and laid hold of one with his right hand, and the other with his left. Samson yelled, "Let me die with the Pelesets!" and he put his back into it, and the house fell on the princes, and on all the people that were in it. The dead who Samson killed in his suicide was more than those he murdered during his life. His brothers and his father's house went down, and they took him, and they went up and buried him between Zorah and Esthaol in the sepulcher of his father Manoah, and he judged Israel twenty years.

Judges: Chapter 17

There was a man from the mountains of Ephraim, and his name was Micah. He said to his mother, "The eleven hundred pieces of silver which you took of yourself, and about which you cursed me, and spoke in my ears, look, the silver is with me. I took it."

His mother said, "Blessed be my son of the Lord."

He restored the eleven hundred pieces of silver to his mother, and his mother said, I had wholly consecrated the money to the Lord out of my hand for my son, to make a graven and a molten image, and now I will restore it to you. But he returned the silver to his mother, and his mother took two hundred pieces of silver and gave them to a silversmith, and he made from it a molten idol, and it was in the house of Micah. The house of Micah was for him, a Temple of God, and he made a vest and teraphim, and he consecrated one of his sons, and he became to him a priest.

In those days there was no king in Israel, and every man did that which was right in his own eyes. There was a young man in the House of Lehem of the tribe of Judah, and he was a Levite, and he was traveling there. The man departed from House of Lehem in a town of Judah to stay in whatever place he might find, and he came as far as Mount Ephraim and stopped at the house of Micah. Micah asked him, "From where have you come?"

He answered him, "I am a Levite from the Temple of Lehem in Judah, and I go to stay in any place I may find."

Micah offered him, "Live with me and be for me a father and a priest, and I will give you ten pieces of silver each year, and a change of clothing, and your living."

The Levite began to live with the man, and the young man was to him as one of his sons. Micah consecrated the Levite, and he became for him a priest, and he was in the house of Micah. Micah said, "Now I know that the Lord will do good for me because a Levite has become my priest."

Judges: Chapter 18

In those days there was no king in Israel, the tribe of Dan wanted for itself an inheritance to inhabit because no inheritance had fallen to it until that day among the tribes of Israel. The sons of Dan sent from their families five men of valor, from Zorah and Esthaol, to spy out the land and to search it. They said to them, "Go and search out the land."

They came as far as the mountains of Ephraim to the house of Micah and they lodged there, in the house of Micah, and they recognized the voice of the young man the Levite, and turned in there, and asked him, "Who brought you in here? And what are you doing in this place? And what have you here?"

He answered them, "Micah hired me, and I became his priest."

They said to him, "Inquire of God, now, whether the path in which we are going will be prosperous."

The priest answered them, "Go in peace. Your way in which you go is before the Lord."

The five men traveled on, and arrived at Laish and saw the people in it living peacefully, and at ease like the Sidonians. There was no one perverting or shaming anything in the land, and no heir extorting their wealth, yet they were far from the Sidonians, and they had no trade with anyone. The five men went to their brothers, to Zorah and Esthaol, and asked their brothers, "Why do you sit here idle?"

They said, "Get up, and let us go up against them, for we have seen the land, and, saw it is very good. Yet you are idle. Don't delay leaving. Enter in and seize the land. When you will go, you will come to a peaceful people, and the land is extensive, but God has given it into your hand. A place where nothing is lacking that the earth provides. They departed there from the families of Dan, from Zorah and Esthaol, six hundred men, equipped with weapons of war. They went up and camped in the village of Ye'arim in Judah. (Therefore that place was called the Camp of Dan, until this day. Look, it is near the village of Ye'arim.)

They went on from there to the mountains of Ephraim and came to the house of Micah. The five men who went to spy out the land of Laish answered, and said to their brothers, "You know that there is in this place, a vest and teraphim, and a molten idol, and now consider what you will do."

They turned aside there, and went into the house of the young man, the Levite, into the Temple of Micah, and asked him how he was. The six hundred Danites who were equipped with their weapons of war stood by the door of the gate. The five men who went to spy out the land went up and entered into the Temple of Micah, and the priest stood. They took the idol, and the vest and teraphim, and the priest asked them, "What are you doing?"

They answered him, "Be silent, lay your hand on your mouth, and come with us, and be for us a father and a priest. Is it better for you to be the priest of the house of one man, or to be the priest of a tribe and house for a family of Israel?"

The heart of the priest was glad, and he took the vest, and teraphim, and molten idol, and went among the people. So they turned and departed, and put their children and their property and their baggage before them. They went some distance from the Temple of Micah, and Micah, and the men in the houses near Micah's Temple, called out, and chased after Dan. Dan turned around, and asked Micah, "What is the matter with you that you have called out?"

Micah said, "You have taken my molten idol which I made, and my priest is gone, and what have I remaining? Yet you ask me, 'Why do you call out?"

The children of Dan said to him, don't let your voice be heard by us, in case angry men attack you, and take away your life, and the lives of your house. The children of Dan went their way, and Micah saw that they were stronger than he was, and he returned to his house. The children of Dan took what Micah had made, and the priest that he had, and they came to Laish, to a quiet and peaceful people, and they slaughtered them with the edge of the sword and burnt the city with fire. There were no survivors, because the city was far from the Sidonians, and they had no trade with other men. It was in the valley of the house of Ereo, that they built the city, and lived in it. They called the name of the city Dan, after the name of Dan their fore-father, who was born to Israel.

(The name of the town had been Hall of the Lion[1] before.)

The children of Dan set up the molten idol for them-selves, and Jonathan son of Gershom son of Manasseh, he and his sons were priests to the tribe of Dan until the time the nation was taken away captive. They set up for themselves the molten idol which Micah made, all the days that the Temple of God was in Shiloh. It was so in those days that there was no king in Israel.

Judges: Chapter 18 Notes

1 Codex Vaticanus: Oylamaes (ΟΥΛΑΜΑΙϹ)

- Codex Alexandrinus: an Laes (ΗΝΛΑΙϹ). Translation: it was Laes

- Aleppo Codex: åwlm lyš (אולם ליש). Translation: but (or Hall of) or lion (or wealth)

- Leningrad Codex: ulam layish (אוּלָם לַיִשׁ). Translation: but (or Hall of) lion (or wealth)

- Targum Jerusalem: veram layish (בְרַם לַיִשׁ). Translation: besides lion (or Leo)

The translators at the library of Alexandria, or the earlier translators of the Aramaic version they worked from interpreted the name differently from the Hebrew translators. The term åwlm (אולם) can be interpreted as 'but,' as the Hebrew translators rendered it, or as 'hall,' or 'salon' as the early Aramaic translators interpreted it. As the Greeks considered it part of the name they transliterated it, meaning they interpreted the Aramaic text as reading 'Hall of Λes.' Either they missed the L (Λ / ל) at the beginning of the name Lysh, or it had been dropped in the Aramaic translation. Reading åwlm lyš (אולם ליש) the way it was read at the Library of Alexandria renders the old name of the town as 'Hall of the Lion' using the unusual but documented translation of lyš (ליש) as 'lion,' or 'Hall that's there,' using the more common interpretation of lyš (ליש). The term lyš does not appear to have had meant 'lion' in early Aramaic, and was probably interpreted as 'the aesh' by the Aramaic translator, who also interpreted Aesh as a proper name, resulting in the translation of 'Hall of Aesh' instead of 'Hall of the Aesh.' As Hall of the Lion is probably the origin of the name, however, that name is imported from the Aleppo Codex.

Judges: Chapter 19

A Levite was traveling along the sides of Mount Ephraim, and he took for himself a concubine from the House of Lehem in Judah. His concubine left him and traveled from him to the house of her father, in the House of Lehem in Judah, and she was there four months. Her husband rose up and went after her, to speak kindly to her, and to restore her to himself. He had a young man with him, and a pair of donkeys. She brought him into the house of her father, and the father of the woman saw him and was very pleased to meet him. His father-in-law, the father of the woman, detained him, and he stayed with him for three days, and they ate and drank, and lodged there. It happened on the fourth day, that they rose early, and he stood up to leave, and the father of the woman said to his son-in-law, "Strengthen your heart with a morsel of bread, and afterward you will go."

They two sat down together and ate and drank, and the father of the woman said to her husband, "Wait now the night, and let your heart be happy."

The man rose to leave, but his father-in-law detained him, and he stayed and lodged there. He rose early in the morning on the fifth day to leave, and the father of the woman said, "Strengthen your, and equip yourself as a soldier until the evening, and the two ate."

The man rose up to leave, he and his concubine, and his young man, but his father-in-law the father of the woman said to him, "Look now, it's late in the day, almost evening, stay here and let your heart rejoice, and you will rise early tomorrow for your journey and you will leave to your home."

But the man would not lodge there, he rose and departed, and came to the area opposite Jebus, (this is Jerusalem,) and there was with him a pair of donkeys saddled, and his concubine was with him. They came as far as Jebus, and the day had advanced, and the young man said to his master, "Come, I beg you, and let us turn aside into this city of the Jebusites, and let us lodge in it."

His master said to him, "We will not turn aside into a strange city, where there are none one of the Israelites. We will pass on as far as Gibeah." He said to his young man, "Come, and let's approach one of the places, and we will lodge in Gibeah or Ramah."

They continued and went on, and the sun set on them near Gibeah, which is in Benjamin. They turned aside there to go into a lodge in Gibeah, and they went in and sat down in the street of the city, and no one took them into a house to lodge. An old man came out of the field from his work in the evening, and the man was from Mount Ephraim, and he stayed in Gibeah, and the men of the place were Benjaminites. He lifted his eyes and saw a traveler in the street of the city, and the old man said to him, "To what place go you, and from where come you?"

He answered him, "We are passing by from House of Lehem in Judah to the sides of Mount Ephraim. I am from there, and I went as far as House of Lehem in Judah, and I am going home, and there is no man to take me into his house. Yet is there straw and food for our donkeys, and bread and wine for me and my handmaid and the young man with your servants, there is no lack of anything."

The old man said, "Peace be to you, only do by no means lodge in the street." He brought him into his house and made room for his donkeys, and they washed their feet and ate and drank.

They were comforting their heart, when look, the lawless men of the city surrounded the house and knocked at the door. They spoke to the old man, the owner of the house, saying, "Bring out the man who came into your house, that we may rape him."

The master of the house came out to them, and said, "No, brothers, do not do wrong, I beg you. After this man has come into my house, do not do this foolishness. Look my daughter a virgin, and the man's concubine, I will bring them out, and humble you them, and do to them that which is good in your eyes, but to this man do not this folly."

But the men would not consent to listen to him, so the man grabbed hold of his concubine, and threw her out to them, and they raped her, and abused her all night until the morning, and let her go when the morning dawned. The woman came back in the early morning and fell at the door of the house where her husband was until it was light. Her husband rose up in the morning, and opened the doors of the house, and went out to go on his journey, and look, the woman his concubine had fallen by the doors of the house, and her hands were on the threshold. He said to her, "Rise, and let us go."

She did not answer, as she was dead. He took her on his donkey and went to his place. He took his sword, and laid hold of his concubine, and divided her into twelve parts, and sent them to every coast of Israel. It was so, that everyone who saw it said, "Such a day as this has not happened nor has been seen from the day of the going up of the Israelites out of the land of Egypt until this day. Take counsel concerning it, and speak."

Judges: Chapter 20

All the Israelites went out, and all the congregation was gathered as one man, from Dan to Beersheba, and in the land of Gilead, to the Lord at Mizpeh. All the tribes of Israel stood before the Lord in the assembly of the people of God, four hundred thousand men who drew a sword. The Benjaminites heard that the Israelites had gone up to Mizpeh, and the Israelites came and said, "Tell us, where did this wickedness take place?"

The Levite, the husband of the woman that was slain, answered and said, "I and my concubine went into Gibeah in Benjamin to lodge. The men of Gibeah rose against me and surrounded the house at night against me. They wished to kill me, and they abused my concubine, and she is dead. I took hold of my concubine, and cut her into pieces, and sent the parts to every border of the inheritance of the Israelites, as they have worked immorally and an abomination in Israel. Look, all you are Israelites. Consider and take counsel here among yourselves."

All the people rose up as one man, saying, "Not one of us will return to his tent, and not one of us will return to his house. Now this is what will be done in Gibeah, we will go up against it by lot. Moreover, we will take ten men for a hundred for all the tribes of Israel, and a hundred for a thousand, and a thousand for ten thousand, to take provisions, for them to come to Gibeah of Benjamin, to do to it according to all the abomination, which they worked in Israel."

All the men of Israel were gathered to the city as one man. The tribes of Israel sent men through the whole tribe of Benjamin, saying, "What is this wickedness that has been worked among you? Now then give up the lawless men that are in Gibeah, and we will put them to death, and purge out wickedness from Israel, but the Benjaminites did not agree to listen to the voice of their brothers the Israelites. The Benjaminites were gathered from their cities to Gibeah, to go out to fight with the Israelites. The Benjaminites from their cities were numbered on that day, twenty-three thousand, every man drawing a sword, besides the inhabitants of Gibeah, who numbered seven hundred chosen men of all the people able to use both hands alike.

All these, could sling stones at a rabbit, and not miss. The men of Israel, other than Benjamin, numbered four hundred thousand men that drew a sword, all these were men of war. They rose and went up to the Temple of El, and asked God, "Who will lead us to fight with the Benjaminites?"

The Lord said, "Judah will go up first as a leader."

The Israelites rose up in the morning and camped near Gibeah. They went out, all the men of Israel, to fight with Benjamin, and engaged with them at Gibeah. The Benjaminites went out from Gibeah, and they destroyed in Israel on that day twenty-two thousand men. The men of Israel strengthened themselves and again engaged in battle in the place where they had engaged on the first day. The Israelites went up, and cried out to the Lord until evening, and inquired of the Lord, saying, "Will we enter battle again with our brothers the Benjaminites?"

The Lord said, "Go up against them."

The Israelites advanced against the Benjaminites on the second day. The Benjaminites went out to meet them from Gibeah on the second day and destroyed another eighteen thousand of the Israelites of those who drew a sword. The Israelites and all the people got up, and went to the Temple of El, and they wept and sat there, before the Lord. They fasted on that day until evening, and offered whole burnt offerings and perfect sacrifices to the Lord, for the box of Lord the god was there in those days. Phinehas the son of Eleazar the son of Aaron stood before it in those days, and the Israelites inquired of the Lord, "Will we again go out to fight with our brothers, the Benjaminites?"

The Lord answered, "Go up, tomorrow and I will give them into your hands."

The Israelites set an ambush near Gibeah, and the Israelites went up against the Benjaminites on the third day and formed up against Gibeah as before. The Benjaminites went out to meet the people, and were all drawn out of the city, and began to attack and kill the people as before in the roads, which go up to the Temple of El, and each from Gibeah was outnumbered by about thirty men of Israel. The Benjaminites said, "They'll fall before us like before."

The Israelites said, "Let us flee, and draw them out from the city into the roads," and they did so. All the men rose up out of their places and engaged in Ba'al Tamar,[1] and those laying in wait of Israel advanced from their place, the cave of Geba.[2] There came against Gibeah ten thousand men were chosen out of all of Israel, and the fight was severe, and they did not know that evil was coming on them. The Lord slaughtered Benjamin before the Israelites, and the Israelites destroyed 25,100 Benjaminites on that day, all those that drew a sword. The Benjaminites saw that they were slaughtered.

The men of Israel gave place to Benjamin because they trusted in the ambuscade which they had prepared against Gibeah. When they retreated, then the layers in wait rose up, and they moved towards Gibeah, and the whole ambush came out, and they struck the city with the edge of the sword. The Israelites had a signal of battle with the layers in wait, that they should send up a signal of smoke from the city. The Israelites saw that the layers in wait had seized Gibeah, and they stood in battle formation, and Benjamin began to kill the wounded ones among the men of Israel, about thirty men, as they said, "Certainly they will fall again before us, as in the first battle."

The signal went up increasingly over the city as a pillar of smoke, and Benjamin looked behind him and saw the destruction of the city rose to the sky. The men of Israel turned back, and the men of Benjamin rushed because they saw that evil had come on them. They ran to the wilderness from before the Israelites and fled, but the battle caught up to them, and they from the cities and destroyed them in the middle of them. They cut down Benjamin, and put an end to them, stopping and trampling them[3] until they came near Gibeah on the east. There fell from Benjamin eighteen thousand men, all these were men of might.

The rest turned and fled to the wilderness to the rock of Rimmon, and the Israelites picked off another five thousand men, and the Israelites chased after them as far as Gedan, and they slaughtered another two thousand of them. All that fell of Benjamin were twenty-five thousand men that drew a sword on that day, all these were men of might. The rest turned and fled to the wilderness to the rock of Rimmon, only six hundred men, and they stayed four months in the rock of Rimmon. The Israelites returned to the Benjaminites and slaughtered them with the edge of the sword from the city of Methla,[4] including the livestock and everything that was found in all the cities, and they burnt with fire the cities they found.

Judges: Chapter 20 Notes

1 Codex Vaticanus: Baalthamar (ΒΑΑΛΘΑΜΑΡ)

- Aleppo Codex: bôl tmr (בעל תמר)

- Leningrad Codex: ba'al Tamar (בַּעַל תָּמָר)

- Targum Jerusalem: Yericho (יְרִיחוֹ). Translation: Jericho

Eusebius reported the existence of a Beth-Tamar in Roman Judea as late as the 4th century AD, however, nothing is known about Baʻal Tamar or Beth-Tamar today. Apparently, nothing was known about is when the Targum Jerusalem was translated as well, as the translator substituted Jericho.

2 Codex Vaticanus: Maaragabe (ΜΑΑΡΑΓΑΒΕ)

- Codex Alexandrinus: dysmôn tês Gabaa (ΔΥCΜΩΝΤΗC ΓΑΒΑΑ). Translation: setting the Gabaa

- Aleppo Codex: môrh gbô (מערה גבע). Translation: cave Geba

- Leningrad Codex: ma'areh-Gava (מַעֲרֵה־גָבַע). Translation: cave of Gava

- Targum Jerusalem: meishar Giv'ata (מֵישַׁר גִּבְעָתָא). Translation: strength (or flat) of Givata

As the Codex Vaticanus includes a transliteration of the term found in the Masoretic Text, that term is imported into this translation as 'cave of Geba.'

3 Codex Vaticanus: cae ediôxan auton apo Noua cata poda autou (ΚΑΙΕΔΙѠΞΑΝΑΥΤΟΝΑΠΟΝΟΥΑΚΑΤΑΠΟΔΑ ΑΥΤΟΥ). Translation: and chased them from Noua and against them

• Codex Alexandrinus: catapausae auton catapausin cae catepatêsan auton (ΚΑΤΑΠΑΥϹΑΙΑΥΤΟΝΚΑΤΑΠΑΥϹΙΝ ΚΑΙΚΑΤΕΠΑΤΗϹΑΝΑΥΤΟΝ). Translation: put an end to them stopped and trampled them

• Aleppo Codex: hrdyphw mnwḥh hdrykhw (הרדיפהו מנוחה הדריכהו). Translation: persecuted them easily guided (or directed, commanded)

• Leningrad Codex: hirdifuhu menuchah hidrichuhu (הִרְדִּיפֻהוּ מְנוּחָה הִדְרִיכֻהוּ). Translation: persecuted them easily guided (or directed, commanded)

• Targum Jerusalem: redafunun mibbeit neyachahon teradunun (רְדָפוּנוּן מִבֵּית נְיָחֲהוֹן טְרָדוּנוּן). Translation: chased them away from inside their inheritance

The translation in the Codex Vaticanus appears to have an error, which was fixed in the Codex Alexandrinus. The Greek translators appear to have mistranslated menuchah (מְנוּחָה), meaning 'easily,' as 'from Noua' (from Noua), therefore the Codex Alexandrius is followed here.

4 Codex Vaticanus: Methla (ΜΕΘΛΑ)

• Codex Alexandrinus: hexês (ΕΞΗϹ). Translation: following

- Aleppo Codex: mtm (מתם). Translation: men

- Leningrad Codex: metom (מְתֹם). Translation: men

- Targum Jerusalem: mikirveihon (מִקִּרְוֵיהוֹן). Translation: original wealth

As all three sources have a different term here, the Codex Vaticanus is followed as it is the oldest.

Judges: Chapter 21

The Israelites swore in Mizpeh, "None of us will give his daughter to a Benjamin as a wife."

The people came to the Temple of El, and sat there until evening before God, and they lifted their voice and cried with a great voice, and said, "Lord the god of Israel! Has this come to pass, That today one tribe should be missing from Israel?"

In the morning the people rose up early, and built an altar, and offered up whole burnt offerings and peace offerings. The Israelites said, "Who of all the tribes of Israel, did not go up in the congregation to the Lord?" as there was a great oath concerning those who did not go up to the Lord in Mizpeh, saying, "He will certainly be put to death."

The Israelites relented towards Benjamin their brothers, and said, "Today one tribe is cut off from Israel. What will we do for wives for the rest that remain? We have sworn by the Lord, not to give them of our daughters as wives."

They asked, "Which man is there the tribes of Israel, who did not go up to the Lord in Mizpeh?"

No man came to the camp from Jabin Gilead to the assembly. The people were counted, and there was not a man there from the inhabitants of Jabin Gilead. The congregation sent twelve thousand of the strongest men, and they ordered, "Go and slaughter the inhabitants of Jabin Gilead with the edge of the sword. Do this to every male, and you will murder every woman that has laid with a man, but the virgins you will keep alive," and they did so.

They found among the inhabitants of Jabin Gilead four hundred young virgins, who had not known a man by lying with him, and they brought them to Shiloh in the land of Canaan. All the congregation sent and spoke to the Benjaminites in the rock Rimmon, and invited them to make peace. Benjamin returned to the Israelites at that time, and the Israelites gave them the women who they had not murdered from the daughters of Jabin Gilead, and they were content. The people repented for Benjamin because the Lord had made a breach in the tribes of Israel.

The elders of the congregation said, "What will we do for wives for those who remain? For the women of Benjamin have been slaughtered."

They said, "There must be an inheritance for them that escaped of Benjamin, or a tribe will be destroyed out of Israel. We will not be able to give them wives from our daughters, because we swore among the Israelites, saying, 'Cursed is he that gives a wife to Benjamin.'"

They said, "Look! Now there is a feast of the Lord from year to year in Shiloh, which is to the north of Bethel, eastward on the road that goes up from Bethel to Shechem, and from the south of Libnah."

They ordered the Benjaminites, saying, "Go and lie in wait in the vineyards, and you will see, and if the daughters of the inhabitants of Shiloh come out to dance in dances, then you will go out of the vineyards and kidnap for yourselves every man a wife of the daughters of Shiloh, and return to the land of Benjamin. When their fathers or their brothers come to dispute with us, then we will say to them, 'Grant them freely to us, for we have not taken each man his wife in battle. Because you did not give to them at the time, you transgressed.'"

The Benjaminites did so, and they took wives according to their number from the dancers who they kidnapped and they went and returned to their inheritance, and built the cities, and lived in them. The Israelites went home at that time every man to his tribe and his families, and they went every man to his inheritance.

In those days there was no king in Israel, every man did that which was right in his own sight.

Ruth: Chapter 1

In the time when the judges ruled, there was a famine in the land, and a man went from the House of Lehem[1] in Judah[2] to stay in the land of Moab[3] with his wife and his two sons. The man's name was Abimelech,[4] and his wife's name Naomi, and the names of his two sons Mahlon and Chilion, Ephrathites[5] from the House of Lahem in Judah who also traveled to the land of Moab and remained there. Abimelech the husband of Naomi died, and she was left with her two sons. They took for themselves as wives, Moabite women. The name of the one was Orpah, and the name of the second Ruth. They lived there for about ten years. Both Mahlon and Chilion also died, and the woman was left without her husband and her two sons.

She rose up with her two daughters-in-law, and they left out of the land of Moab, for she heard in the country of Moab that the Lord[6] had visited his people to give them bread. She left the place where she was, and her two daughters-in-law with her, and they traveled by road to return to the land of Judah. Naomi said to her daughters-in-law, "Return now, return each to the house of her mother. The Lord deal mercifully with you, as you have dealt with the dead, and with me. The Lord grant you that you may find rest, each of you in the house of her husband," and she kissed them.

They lifted their voice and wept. They said to her, "We will return with you to your people."

Naomi said, "Return now, my daughters. Why do you go with me? Have I more sons in my womb to be your husbands? Turn now, my daughters, for I am too old to be married. As I said, 'Suppose I were married and should carry sons, would you wait for them until they should be grown? Or would you refrain from being married for their sake?' No, my daughters, I am sad for you, that the hand of the Lord has gone out against me."

They lifted their voice and wept again, and Orpah kissed her mother-in-law and returned to her people, but Ruth continued to follow her. Naomi said to Ruth, "Look, your sister-in-law has returned to her people and to her gods, now turn also and follow after your sister-in-law."

Ruth replied, "Don't ask me to leave you, or to turn from following you. Wherever you go, I will go, and wherever you lodge, I will lodge. Your people will be my people, and your god will be my god. Wherever you die, I will die, and there I will be buried. The Lord do so for me, and more also, if I leave you. Only death will divide me and you."

Naomi, seeing that she was determined to go with her, stopped speaking to her about it. They both traveled until they came to the Temple of Lahem, and it came to pass, when they arrived at the Temple of Lahem, that all the city rang with them, and they asked, "Is this Naomi?"

She said to them, "No, do not call me Naomi. Call me Bitter, as Shaddayin[7] has dealt very bitterly with me. I went out full, and the Lord has brought me back empty. Why do you call me Naomi, when the Lord has humbled me and Shaddayin has afflicted me?"

So Naomi and Ruth the Moabitess, her daughter-in-law, returned from the country of Moab, and they arrived at the Temple of Lahem at the beginning of barley harvest.

Ruth: Chapter 1 Notes

1 Codex Vaticanus: Baethleem (ΒΑΙΘΛΕΕΜ)

• Codex Alexandrinus: Bêthleem (ΒΗΘΛΕΕΜ)

• Septuagint ms. 376: Bithleem (Βιθλόόμ)

• Septuagint ms. 131: Bêthlaeem (Βιθλάιόμ)

• Aleppo Codex: byt lḥm (בית לחם). Translation: house (or temple, abode) of Lehem (or bread)

• Leningrad Codex: beit Lechem (בֵּית לֶחֶם). Translation: house (or temple, abode) of Lehem (or bread)

• Vetus Latina: Bethlem

• Targum on Ruth: beit Lechem (בֵּית לֶחֶם). Translation: house (or temple, abode) of Lehem (or bread)

2 Codex Vaticanus: Iouda (ΙΟΥΔΑ). Translation: Judah

• Septuagint ms. 119: Ioudaeas (ιουΔΑ φΑc). Translation: Judea

• Aleppo Codex: Yhwdh (יהודה). Translation: Judah

• Leningrad Codex: Yehudah (יְהוּדָה). Translation: Judah

• Targum on Ruth: Yehudah (יְהוּדָה). Translation: Judah

Judah was an iron age kingdom in southern modern Israel and the Palestinian West Bank between approximately 930 and 586 BC, which indicates the story was likely written during this era.

The time period mentioned when the judges ruled, dates the story to earlier. Based on the later reference to Naomi being the mother of Obed, the grandfather of King David, the story is set around 1100 BC.

3 Codex Vaticanus: Môab (ⲘⲱⲀⲃ). Translation: Moab

- Aleppo Codex: Mwâb (מוֹאָב). Translation: Moab

- Leningrad Codex: Mo'av (מוֹאָב). Translation: Moab

- Targum on Ruth: Mo'av (מוֹאָב). Translation: Moab

Moab was a kingdom in modern Jordan, on the east shore of the Dead Sea from sometime before King Ramesses II of Egypt, who recorded them as a country he conquered during his third Syrian campaign in 1291 BC.

4 Codex Vaticanus: Abimelech (Ⲁⲃⲉⲓⲙⲥⲁⲉⲭ)

- Codex Alexandrinus: Alimelec (Ⲁⲁⲓⲙⲉⲁⲉⲕ)

- Codex Basiliano-Vaticanus: Elimelech (ⲉⲁⲓⲙⲉⲁⲉⲭ)

- Septuagint ms. 241: Alimelech (Ἀλιμέλόχ)

- Septuagint ms. 243: Ailimelech (Ἀιλιμέλόχ)

- Aleppo Codex: Âlymlk (אלימלך)

- Leningrad Codex: Elimelech (אֱלִימֶלֶךְ)

- Targum on Ruth: Elimelech (אֱלִימֶלֶךְ)

This name does not survive in this verse among the Dead Sea Scrolls, however, has survived in later verses.

• Dead Sea Scroll 4QRuthª: ålymlk (אלימלך)

There is no obvious reason the Hasmoneans would have changed the name of Abimelech to Elimelech, unless it was to disassociate King David's house from circa 1000 BC, from the earlier house of King Abimelech, the first King of Israel, circa 1267 to 1264 BC. These two Abimelechs cannot be the same person, as their stories have nothing in common, and they lived a century apart, nevertheless, the names are different in the Septuagint's version of Ruth, translated circa 225 BC and the oldest pre-Masoretic version of Ruth, the Dead Sea Scroll 4QRuthª, dates to the Hasmonean Dynasty (140-37 BC). It is possible that the Hasmoneans did not change the name and there were two versions of the texts in circulation before the Greeks translated the text, or, that the Greeks mistranslated the name.

5 LXX 236: Ephraam (Εφρααμ)

• LXX 29: Ephrathaeoe (Εφραθαιοι)

• LXX 54: Ephranthaeoe (Εφρανθαιοι)

• Aleppo Codex: Åfrtym (אפרתים)

• Leningrad Codex: Efratim (אֶפְרָתִים)

• Targum on Ruth: Efratin rabbanin (אֶפְרָתִין רַבָּנִין).
Translation: Ephramite nobles

- Dead Sea Scroll 4QRuthª: Åfrtym (אגרתים)

- Vetus Latina: euphratei

Ephratha (ЄФΡΛΘΛ) / Efratah (אֶפְרָתָה) was listed as the former name of Bethlehem in the Torah. The name appears to be the Egyptian name, erperte (𓉐𓏏𓊃𓅓𓇯), which translates as 'temple of bread, a direct translation of the Canaanite name byt lhm (𐤁𐤉𐤕 𐤋𐤇𐤌). The same region is later known as the land of Ephriam (אֶפְרַיִם) during the early iron age, and part of the Kingdom of Samaria until it was conquered by Assyrian war in 723 BC. While LXX 236 reads Ephriam, the rest of the sources support the reading or Ephrathiam, indicating that these were the remnants of the Egyptized Bethlehemites that would have still been present in the region in the era the book is set in. This suggests the book of Ruth dates back to the early iron age.

6 Greek: c̄s̄ (ΚC). Translation: lord

- Dead Sea Scroll 4QRuthª: Yhwh (יהוה).

- Aleppo Codex: Yhwh (יהוה)

- Leningrad Codex: Yehvah (יְהֹוָה)

- Targum on Ruth: Yeyah (??). Translation: Yahw

The Septuagint's version of the Ruth was translated before 200 BC, as it was carried south by the Beta Israel community, who left Egypt for Kush (modern Sudan) during the Jewish Rebellion against the Ptolemys in 200 BC. This means it predates the Hasmonean redaction and contains the term Lord (Κύριος) instead of Iaw (Ιαω).

There are no surviving early fragments of the Septuagint's Ruth that include the name, suggesting the word in the Aramaic version of Exodus was Ădōnāy, which meant 'lord' and was also the name of a god in the Canaanite religion, especially in the region around Baalbek, in modern Lebanon. Like the Samaritan Yahw, Adonay was the son of Asherah, suggesting that the Aramaic term in the text the Greek translation was made from used the name Adonay.

The Aramaic sections of Masoretic Daniel that were not translated into Hebrew maintain the term adonai ha'elohim (אֲדֹנָי הָאֱלֹהִים), meaning the 'Lord the gods' where the Septuagint has 'Lord the god' (Κύριον τὸν θεὸν), however, the Hebrew sections have Yehvah elohim (יְהוָה אֱלֹהִים) where the Septuagint has 'Lord the god,' suggesting the Greek more accurately reflects the Aramaic source texts than the Hebrew translation. According to Sanhedrin (103b) tractate in the Talmud, King Manasseh was blamed for removing the name, however, as his grandson Josiah 'restored' the Torah circa 625 BC, one would expect that he would have restored the name as well, if it had have been in Exodus to begin with. Furthermore, the early Torah appears to have already been translated into Aramaic during the era of Manasseh's father king Hezekiah, suggesting that he removed the name during his religious reforms.

As the original translation of Ruth does not appear to have included the name, the term 'Lord' is used in this translation.

Lord (Ba'al and Adon) were commonly used in ancient Canaan as titles of the various Canaanite gods, and early Israelites appear to have used the terms the same way themselves. In this context, the Lord in question is Lord Lehem, the Canaanite god of fertility, grains, and rebirth. The limited amount of information that survives about him, suggests he was similar to Osiris and Dionysus, meaning he would have been a precursor to Lord Sabaoth.

7 Greek: icanos (ικανος). Translations: capable (or able, competent, skillful, fit, potent, efficient, apt, shifty)

- LXX 29: ischyros (ισχυβος). Translations: strong (or powerful, mighty)

- Aleppo Codex: šdy (שׁדי). Translation: demons (or phantoms, demonic, ghoulish, devilish)

- Leningrad Codex: Shaddai (שַׁדָּי). Translation: (or demons, phantoms, demonic, ghoulish, devilish)

- Targum on Ruth: Shaddai (שַׁדָּי). Translation: (or powerful)

- Vetus Latina: deus. Translation: god

In the Septuagint, the term El Shaddai was directly transliterated as theos Saddai (θεος Σαδδαι) once in Ezekiel, and therefore the term must have been in the Aramaic texts the Greeks used to translate Ezekiel, however, in the other books of the Septuagint, the term 'almighty' (παντοκρατορος) appears where the Masoretic Texts have Shaddai. Šdyn

(𐤔𐤃𐤉), generally anglicized as Shaddayin, was a Moabite god in the 800s BC, as evidenced by the Deir Alla Inscription (or KAI 312), which was found during an excavation at Deir 'Alla, Jordan, and described Balaam as the prophet of the Elohin and Shaddayin, believed to be Moabite translations of 'Elohim' and 'Shaddai.'

In the Book of Ruth, Shaddai is placed in opposition to the Lord God of Israel, which implies the name was left in the Judahite version of Ruth after the Hasmonean redaction as it was viewed as a reference to the Moabite god, who 'dealt very bitterly' with Naomi when she was in Moab. The Greek and Hebrew translations often differ in regards to the name or title Shaddai, suggesting that the Aramaic and Canaanite (Judahite or Samaritan) source texts they worked from differed in regards to this word. The term was omitted throughout Cosmic Genesis, suggesting that when the word was first encountered the Greeks did not know how to interpret it. It is equally possible that it was the Aramaic translator who had omitted it, however, it was almost certainly in the Canaanite version the translator worked from, as it is used consistently in the rest of Genesis, and is mentioned again when Moses god's name Ān is introduced in the Septuagint's Exodus. The cause of the confusion over the term Shaddai, is likely due to the difference between the meaning of the word in Canaanite versus Aramaic.

In Akkadian cuneiform, which was adopted as the written script by many cultures, the term was ^{deity}Šēdu (✳𐎁), however, it referred to a 'protective spirit' or 'lesser god.' In the later Aramaic language, the word became šydå (ΝΊ^Ʊ), meaning 'demon' in the classical sense, as a type of muse or nymph. Whereas in Canaanite, šd (ᕁᏔ) took on a different meaning, generally interpreted as 'powerful' by the Early Classical Era, which is likely where the Greeks ultimately derived the term 'omnipotent' (παντοκράτορος), which was used later in the Septuagint where the Masoretic Text generally uses the term Shaddai.

This alternate interpretation of the šd (ᕁᏔ) in Canaanite is likely due to the Egyptian New Kingdom era rule over Canaan, when Shed (𓆷𓂝𓏤, transliteration: šd), was worshiped in the region. Shed, who was often referred to as 'the savior,' was virtually identical to the earlier Canaanite god Resheph who was largely suppressed after the fall of the Hyksos dynasty. In the Masoretic Book of Job, Eliphaz referred to humanity as the 'sons of Resheph' (בני-רשף) instead of the 'sons of Adam,' and then refers god as šdy (שדי).

This usage is consistent throughout Masoretic Job, indicating that at some point the name Resheph was updated to Shaddai, likely during the New Kingdom era, when Resheph worship was suppressed due to his associated with the earlier Hyksos dynasty. During the early New Kingdoms era, holy texts about Resheph would have been updated to Shed (𓆷𓂝𓏤), which would have been transliterated into Canaanite using the Akkadian Cuneiform script in the late New Kingdom era as ^{deity}Šēdu (𒀭𒁲), before being translated into Canaanite using the Phoenician script in the early iron age as šdy (𐤔𐤃𐤉), resulting in the confusing 'god of demons'

(𐤔𐤃𐤉) in Aramaic. In this particular verse, 'capable' (ικανος) appears to be a translation of a word similar to šdy (שׁדי), but not actually šdy, or 'omnipotent' (παντοκράτορος) would have been used, as in other books of the Septuagint, and therefore the Moabite version of the name, Shaddayin, is used in this translation.

Ruth: Chapter 2

Naomi had a friend, an acquaintance of her husband, and the man was a mighty man of the families of Abimelech. His name was Boaz. Ruth the Moabitess said to Naomi, "Let me go now to the field, and I will glean from the ears behind whichever man will let me."

She replied to her, "Go, daughter."

She went and gleaned in the field behind the reapers and she happened by chance to come on a portion of the land of Boaz of the families of Abimelech, and Boaz came from the Temple of Lahem and said to the reapers, "The Lord be with you."

They said to him, "The Lord bless you."

Boaz asked his servant who was in charge of the reapers, "Whose is this girl?"

His servant who was in charge of the reapers answered and said, "It is the Moabite girl who returned with Naomi out of the land of Moab. She asked, 'I beg you, let me glean and gather among the sheaves after the reapers,' and she came and worked from morning until evening, and did not rest even a little in the field."

Boaz said to Ruth, "Have you not heard, my daughter? Don't go to glean in another field and don't leave here. Stay close with my girls, and watch the field where my men reap, and go after them. Look, I have ordered the young men not to touch you, and when you thirst, then you may go to the vessels, and drink of that which the young men will have drawn."

She fell on her face, and did reverence to the ground, and said to him, "How is it that I have found grace in your eyes, that you should take notice of me, when I am a foreigner?"

Boaz answered her, "It has been told to me how you have dealt with your mother-in-law after the death of your husband, and how you left your father and your mother, and the land of your birth, and came to a people who you did not know before. The Lord repay your work, may a full reward be given you of the Lord God of Israel, to whom you have come to trust under his wings."

She said, "Let me find grace in your sight, my lord, because you have comforted me, and because you have spoken kindly to your handmaid, and look, I will be one of your servants."

Boaz said to her, "Now it is time to eat. Come here, and you will eat of the bread, and you will dip your food in the vinegar."

Ruth sat by the side of the reapers, and Boaz handed her a meal and she ate until she was satisfied and left. She rose up to glean and Boaz ordered his young men,

"Let her even among the sheaves, and do not reproach her. You, carry it for her and drop for her some of that which is piled up. Let her eat and glean, and don't rebuke her."

So she gleaned in the field until evening and beat out all that she had gleaned, and it was about a bushel of barley. She picked it up and went into the city. Her mother-in-law saw what she had gleaned, and Ruth brought out and gave her the food which she had left after she had been satisfied. Her mother-in-law said to her, "Where have you gleaned today, and where have you worked? Blessed be he that took notice of you."

Ruth told her mother-in-law where she had worked, and said, "The name of the man with who I worked today is Boaz."

Naomi said to her daughter-in-law, "Blessed is he by the Lord because he has not failed in his mercy with the living and with the dead. The man is a close relative to us, he is one of our relations."

Ruth said to her mother-in-law, "Yes, he also told me, 'Keep close to my girls, until the men will have finished all my reaping.'"

Naomi said to Ruth her daughter-in-law, 'It is well, daughter, that you went out with his girls, so they will not meet you in another field."

Ruth joined herself to the girls of Boaz to glean until they had finished the barley harvest and the wheat harvest.

Ruth: Chapter 3

She lodged with her mother-in-law, and Naomi her mother-in-law said to her, "My daughter, should I not seek rest for you, that it may be well with you? Now is not Boaz our relative, with whose girls you were? Look, he winnows barley this night on the floor. Wash and anoint yourself, and get dressed and go up to the threshing floor. Do not show yourself to the man until he has done eating and drinking. It will come to pass when he lies down, that you will watch the place where he lies down, and will come and lift up the covering of his feet, and will lie down. He will tell you what to do."

Ruth said to her, "I will do all that you say, She went down to the threshing floor, and did according to all that her mother-in-law told her. Boaz ate and drank, and his heart was glad, and he came to lie down by the side of the heap of grain, and she sneaked to him and lifted the covering off his feet. It was past midnight and the man was amazed, and troubled, and saw a woman laying at his feet."

He asked, "Who are you?"

She answered, "I am your handmaid Ruth, spread your skirt over your handmaid, for you are a near relative."

Boaz said, "Blessed are you by the Lord God,[1] my daughter, for you have made your latter kindness greater than the former, in that you don't chase after young men, whether they are poor or rich. Now don't be afraid, my daughter, whatever you will say I will do to you, for all the tribe of my people know that you are a virtuous woman. Now I am truly related to you, nevertheless, there is a relative nearer than I. Lodge here for the night, and it will be in the morning, if he will do the duty of a relative to you, well let him do it, but if he will not do the duty of a relative to you, I will do the relative's duty to you, as the Lord lives. Lie down until the morning."

She lay at his feet until the morning, and she rose up before the sun rose, and Boaz said, "Let it not be known that a woman came into the floor."

He said to her, "Bring the apron that is on you," and she held it, and he measured six measures of barley and put them on her, and she went into the city. Ruth went to her mother-in-law, and she said to her, "My daughter!" and Ruth told her all that the man had done to her.

She said to her, "He gave me these six measures of barley, as he said to me, 'Don't go empty to your mother-in-law.'"

She replied, "Sit still, my daughter, until you will know how the matter will fall out. The man will not rest today until the matter is accomplished.

Ruth: Chapter 3 Notes

1 Codex Vaticanus: c̄o ̄thô (ⲕ̄ⲱⲟ̄ⲩ). Translation: Lord God

• Codex Alexandrinus: cyriô (ⲕⲨⲣⲓⲱ). Translation: Lord

• LXX 106: Cyriô tô theô (Ⲕⲩⲣⳝⲱ ⲧⲱ θⳝ). Translation: Lord the god

• LXX 29: Theô (θⳝ). Translations: God

• Aleppo Codex: Yhwh (יהוה)

• Leningrad Codex: Yhvah (יְהֹוָה)

• Targum on Ruth: Yeyah (יְיָ). Translation: Yahw

The Septuagint's version of the Ruth was translated circa 225 BC, before the Hasmonean redaction, and contains the term Lord God (Κυριω Θεω) instead of the name Yhvah / Yahw. The Aramaic sections of Masoretic Daniel that were not translated into Hebrew maintain the term adonai ha'elohim (אֲדֹנָי הָאֱלֹהִים), meaning the 'Lord the gods' where the Septuagint has 'Lord the god' (Κύριον τὸν θεὸν), however, the Hebrew sections have Yehvah elohim (יְהֹוָה אֱלֹהִים) where the Septuagint has 'Lord the god,' suggesting the Greek more accurately reflects the Aramaic source texts than the Hebrew translation.

According to the Sanhedrin (103b) tractate in the Talmud, King Manasseh was blamed for removing the name, however, as his grandson Josiah 'restored' the Torah circa 625 BC, one would expect that he would have restored the name as well, if it had have been in Exodus to begin with. Furthermore, the early Torah appears to have already been translated into Aramaic during the era of Manasseh's father king Hezekiah, suggesting that he removed the name during his religious reforms.

As the original text of Ruth was almost certainly written in Phoenician (Paleo-Hebrew), the original term was probably Ådn Ålm (𐤀𐤋𐤃𐤀 𐤌𐤋𐤀). Ådn Ålm was a Canaanite epithet for El, found in the Ugaritic Texts from the 1300s BC. In the polytheistic Canaanite religion, the term translates as 'Father of the gods' as El was the father of the 70 Elohim (gods) and creator of the world in the Canaanite religion. The term 'father of the gods' subsequently became Lord God in the Aramaic translation made in the Babylonian or Persian era, before being replaced by Yehvah in the Hasmonean dynasty. According to several ancient Hebrew scriptures, El had a major temple in Shiloh, the capital of ancient Samaria, which Jacob built in the Book of Genesis. El is also mentioned in later books of the Septuagint and appears to have been one of the main gods worshiped by the ancient Israelites, as well as other Canaanites. As Κυριω Θεω translates directly as Lord God, that term is used in this translation.

Ruth: Chapter 4

Boaz went up to the gate and sat there, and watched until the relative passed by, of whom Boaz had spoken. Boaz said to him, "Turn aside, and sit here," and he turned aside and sat down. Boaz called ten men of the elders of the city, and said, "Sit here," and they sat down.

Boaz said to the relative, "The matter regards the portion of the field which was our brother Abimelech's which was given to Naomi when she returned out of the land of Moab. I said, 'I will inform you. Buy it before those who sit, and before the elders of my people. If you will redeem it, redeem it, but if you will not redeem it, tell me, and I will know, for there is no one beside you to do the duty of a relative, and I am next after you."

He replied, "I am here, and I will redeem it."

Boaz said, "In the day of your buying the field of the hand of Naomi and of Ruth the Moabitess the wife of the deceased, you must also buy her, to raise up the name of the dead on his inheritance."

The relative said, "Will I not be able to redeem it for myself, in case I damage my own inheritance? You redeem my right for yourself, as I will not be able to redeem it."

This was the ordinance in Israel for redemption in former times, and for a bargain, to confirm every word, a man removed his shoe and gave it to his neighbor that redeemed his right. This was a testimony in Israel. The relative said to Boaz, "Buy my right for yourself, and he took off his shoe and gave it to him."

Boaz said to the elders and to all the people, "You are this day witnesses, that I have bought all that was Abimelech's, and all that belonged to Chilion and Mahlon, of the hand of Naomi. Moreover, I have bought for myself as wife Ruth the Moabitess, the wife of Mahlon, to raise up the name of the dead on his inheritance, so the name of the dead will not be destroyed from among his brothers, and from the tribe of his people. You are on this day witnesses."

All the people who were in the gate said, "We are witnesses," and the elders said, "The Lord make your wife who goes into your house, as Rachel and as Leah, who both together built the house of Israel, and worked mightily in Ephrath, and there will be a name for you in the Temple of Lahem. Let your house be as the house of Pharez, who Tamar carried for Judah, of the seed which the Lord will give you of this handmaid. Boaz took Ruth, and she became his wife, and he went into her, and the Lord gave her conception, and she carried a son.

The woman said to Naomi, "Blessed is the Lord, who has not allowed a redeemer to fail you this day, even to make your name famous in Israel. He will be for you a restorer of your mind, and one to cherish your old age. For your daughter-in-law which has loved you, who is better to you than seven sons, has born him."

Naomi took the child and laid it on her chest, and became a nurse to it. The neighbors gave it a name, saying, "A son has been born to Naomi," and they called his name Obed. This is the father of Jesse the father of David.

These are the generations of Pharez:

Pharez fathered Hezron,

Hezron fathered Ram,

Ram fathered Amminadab,

Amminadab fathered Nahshon,

Nahshon fathered Salmon,

Salmon fathered Boaz,

Boaz fathered Obed.

Obed fathered Jesse,

and Jesse fathered David.

Septuagint Manuscripts

The following is a list of the Septuagint manuscripts referenced in the notes for this book.

LXX A (Codex Alexandrinus) is dated to the 5th century. It is currently located at the British Library (Royal 1 D. VIII) in London.

LXX B (Codex Vaticanus) is dated to the 4th century. It is currently located at the Vatican Library (Gr. 1209) in Vatican City.

LXX 29 is dated to the 14th century. It is currently located at the Marciana Library (Gr. 2) in Venice.

LXX 119 is dated to the 10th century. It is currently located at the National Library of France (Gr. 7) in Paris.

LXX 106 is dated to the 14th century. It is currently located at the Biblioteca Comunale Ariostea (187 I-III) in Ferrara.

LXX 131 is dated to the 10th century. It is currently located at the Austrian National Library (Theol. Gr. 57) in Vienna.

LXX 241 is dated to the 17th century. It is currently located at the British Museum (Harley MS 7522 A) in London.

LXX 376 is dated to the 15th century. It is currently located at the Royal Library (Y (Griech.)-II-5) in El Escorial.

Alternative Translations

The following is a list of alternative translations that were used for comparative analysis.

The Aleppo Codex is dated to circa 920 AD. For centuries it was housed at the Central Synagogue of Aleppo, from which its name is derived. It was the oldest known complete copy of the Hebrew scriptures used within Judaism until 1947, when it was seized and divided among Jewish families during anti-Jewish riots in Aleppo. The sections that have resurfaced are currently at the Israel Museum in Jerusalem. Approximately 40% is still missing.

The Leningrad Codex is dated to 1008 (or 1009) AD. It is currently located at the National Library of Russia (Firkovich B 19 A) in St. Petersburg. The Leningrad Codex is the oldest complete copy of the Hebrew scriptures used within Judaism.

Targum Jerusalem has historically been misidentified as the Targum Jonathan, and is commonly called the Targum Pseudo-Jonathan in academic literature. Its oldest name is the Targum Jerusalem, which is used here. It is written in Palestinian-Aramaic, and generally dated to sometime between the 4th and 11th centuries. Some scholars believe it originated in the 4th century, and was modified after the Islamic conquest of Palestine, as it includes some Arabic names generally found in Islamic sources. It existed before the crusades, as it was documented at the time.

The Targum on Ruth was published in the 1516 edition of the Mikraot Gedolot, a Hebrew language translation and commentary on the Hebrew Bible, that included Aramaic targums on the various books. The origin of the Targum on Ruth is unknown, however, it is accepted as being composed earlier than 600 AD.

The Vetus Latina are the old Latin translations of the Septuagint and other Israelite texts that predate Jerome's Latin Orthodox Bible in the 5th century. Some of the texts appear to have been translated directly from Aramaic or Hebrew source texts, however, most appear to have been translations from the Greek translations.

Dead Sea Scrolls

The following is a list of the Dead Sea Scrolls mentioned in the notes for this book. Most are held by the Israel Museum in Jerusalem.

DSS 4Q49 (4QJudg^a) is dated to the Hasmonean Dynasty in Judea (140 to 37 BC).

DSS 4Q50 (4QJudg^b) is dated to the Hasmonean Dynasty in Judea (140 to 37 BC).

DSS 4Q104 (4QRuth^a) is dated to the Hasmonean Dynasty in Judea (140 to 37 BC).

Also Available

ALSO AVAILABLE

- Octateuch: The Original Orit

ENOCH AND METATRON SERIES:
- Books of Enoch Collection

- Books of Enoch and Metatron Collection

- Books of Metatron Collection

- Secrets of Enoch

OTHER TRANSLATIONS:
- Apocalypses of Ezra

- Arabic Maccabees

- Life of Adam and Eve

- Memories of the New Kingdom

- Septuagint's Esther and the Vetus Latina Esther

- Septuagint's Ezekiel and the Ba'al Cycle

- Septuagint's Job and the Testament of Job

- Septuagint's Proverbs and the Wisdom of Amenemope

- The Amarna Letters

- Testaments of the Patriarchs Collection

- Tobit and Ahikar

- Ugaritic Texts: Ba'al Cycle

- Wisdom of Ahikar